MW01518568

The Little Red Book

THE ORIGINAL 12 STEP BOOK

ID 826 8554 7726

PASSWORD 723 098

THE ORIGINAL 12 STEP BOOK

AN INTERPRETATION
of
THE TWELVE STEPS
of the
ALCOHOLICS ANONYMOUS PROGRAM

ISBN: 1-4-9979-118-6

ISBN: 978-1-4997-9118-1 (CreateSpace-Assigned)

I would like to dedicate this book to the nameless people of A.A. who contributed to it. In grateful appreciation to Dr Bob, for making this book the first suggested de-facto standard for doing the twelve steps. And to Ed Webster who stood on the shoulders of the old timers and created this masterpiece of straightforwardness and simplicity.

I would like to acknowledge John Moser,
for encouraging me to republish The Little Red Book

Introduction

"The little Red Book" was the first guide to understanding and working the 12 steps. We do not know how many people contributed to this book. Early recovering alcoholics developed pamphlets to help with each step. They were copied and passed around to different groups within A.A. It is believed that the origin of the pamphlets were in the West and the Midwest groups. Ed Webster through his publishing company (Coll-Webb Co) was the first to produce "The little Red book" in a consolidated form. We are told that Dr Bob gave this book to newcomers to help them to work the 12 steps. Dr. Bob thought it was the best description of how to work the steps that had ever been written. He sent copies of it all over the U.S. and Canada with his recommendation. Dr Bob Also convinced A.A. world headquarters in New York to offer this book for sale as tool for A, A. members. There were several editions of the book, with each edition having clarifications and changes made. The book eventually went out of favor when Bill W. collaborated on the writing of the current A.A. 12 and 12. Soon after the Twelve Steps and Twelve Traditions was published, A.A. stopped offering This Little Red (Golden) Book.

The purpose for republishing this book is to provide today's Members of A.A. with an indispensable tool for working the program. The Little Red book served the early A.A. members

Well. It was created by them, and It gave an in depth guide to the steps mentioned in The Big Book.

May this twice Born book, help the countless millions on the path of recovery with the twelve steps.

In fellowship and with blessings

Tuchy Palmieri

CONTENTS

Page

INTRODUCTION

THE TWELVE STEPS

STEP ONE

STEP TWO

STEP THREE

STEP FOUR

STEP FIVE

STEPS SIX AND SEVEN

STEPS EIGHT AND NINE

STEP TEN

STEP ELEVEN

STEP TWELVE

APPENDIX

WORKING WITH OTHERS

WE DON'T HAVE TO—BUT . . .

AUTHOR'S NOTE

The little Red Book evolved from a series of notes originally prepared for "Twelve Step" suggestions to A.A. beginners. It lends supplementary aid to the study of the book, "Alcoholics Anonymous," and contains many helpful topics for discussion meetings. Its distribution is prompted by a desire to "Carry the Message to Alcoholics" in appreciation of our reprieve from alcoholic death.

Many groups, in meeting the A.A. need for instruction of new members, have adopted this brief summarization of the A.A. Recovery Program expounded in the Big Book, "Alcoholics Anonymous," as an outline for study of that book. Worthwhile results have followed the inauguration of weekly classes devoted to guidance of new members in their quest for a better understanding of the "12 Steps" as a way of life.

These classes, directed by qualified members, have created a solidarity of understanding within our Fellowship. They have brought a closer adherence to the Big Book, better understanding and application of its philosophy, more effective sponsorship and a much higher ratio of sobriety among our members.

DEDICATION

We sincerely dedicate this interpretation to

BILL & DR. BOB

in appreciation of their tireless efforts and inspiration in making possible a *Way of Life* by which alcoholics everywhere can recover from alcoholism.

The endless thousands who have recovered from this illness and those who are yet to be helped will ever be indebted to the founders of *Alcoholics Anonymous* for the unselfish service they have rendered all alcoholics.

We believe our founders were inspired by a *Power Greater than Themselves* as they pioneered the Alcoholics Anonymous Fellowship, wrote and edited the book, "Alcoholics Anonymous" and exemplified daily the spiritual philosophy of its recovery program.

INTRODUCTION

The introduction to the Twelve Steps of the Alcoholics Anonymous program is humbly offered to all alcoholic men and women whose "lives have become unmanageable" because of their powerlessness over alcohol.

The purpose of this interpretation is to help members quickly work out an acceptable 24-hour schedule of A.A. living. Its subject matter is founded on basic information from our book, "Alcoholics Anonymous."

All supplementary matter is based on practical experience from the lives of fellow alcoholics who have found peace of mind and contented sobriety by a planned way of spiritual life set forth in the book, "Alcoholics Anonymous."

We too often fail to realize the extent to which we are physically, mentally and spiritually ill, and through ignorance dwarf parts of our program to suit our own distorted viewpoint.

It is obvious that much good can be accomplished by sharing with others the fund of knowledge which successful older members have gained by experience. The purpose of this introduction and the object of this interpretation is toward that end.

As uncontrolled drinkers, few of us realized the danger of our position or the great extent to which the illness alcoholism had damaged and deteriorated our minds and bodies. Nor did we realize the full significance and effectiveness of our simple program without the help and cooperation of understanding members who had arrested their alcoholism.

The A.A. program by which we effect our recovery is extremely simple. It needs little interpretation in itself. It will work if we live it. The only barriers to success are reservations, indifference and brain damage.

A.A. is not a religion. It is not accountable to organized religion, medicine or psychology. It has, however, drawn therapeutic virtues from them all, moulding them into a "Design for Living" by which we live in contented sobriety and are restored to service and respect in society.

The A.A. program is designed for uncontrolled drinkers who sincerely desire permanent sobriety and are willing to go to any lengths to get it. It invariably fails alcoholics who would educate themselves to control their drinking. Men or women interested in temporary sobriety or in controlling their drinking are not ready for this program.*

The ability to be honest is a necessary requirement for rehabilitation. Willingness to get well, and belief in a *Power Greater than Ourselves* are also essential to success.

Spiritual concepts must be embraced, but again we say they do not involve organized religion and although we must believe in this *Higher Power* yet it is our privilege to interpret it in accordance with our own understanding.*

The alcoholics who have recovered through the Alcoholics Anonymous Fellowship internationally disprove the age-old conviction that all alcoholics are untrustworthy, and that they are destined to remain hopeless drunken sots. Thousands upon thousands have disproved this, and hundreds of new alcoholics are daily proving that by living the A.A. philosophy, alcoholism can be arrested.

Permanent sobriety is the aim of the A.A. philosophy, but that in itself is not enough.

* Note paragraph 2, page 44, in the book, "ALCOHOLICS ANONYMOUS."
* Read page 59 in the book "ALCOHOLICS ANONYMOUS."

We should become humble and appreciative; contented, happy and responsible.

The Twelve Steps of the A.A. program have provided us with a sound and proved means of recovery; we have yet to meet an alcoholic who, honestly desirous of arresting his alcoholism, and conscientiously living the Twelve Steps, did not recover.

It is true certain drinkers have not succeeded. A few of the reasons for their failures are listed.

1. Those who see in alcoholism a moral problem rather than an illness.

2. Some had suffered brain injury from alcohol. (Deterioration.)

3. Some failed because they were dope addicts — they drank, yes—but alcohol was not their basic problem.

4. Some were forced into the movement; they lacked sincerity, so did not last.

5. Some were heavy drinkers, but not alcoholics. They were not mentally or physically *one of the seven in every one thousand* adults who are alcoholics.

6. Occasionally there has been an atheist who is unwilling to accept the spiritual concept which underlies the A.A. program. (See Appendix 2 of A.A. Book.)

7. The alcoholic who is "constitutionally dishonest" has little chance.* He cannot be honest with himself.

8. Some sought our help to appease their wives, their employers, or a judge; others to avoid impending evils that prolonged drinking develops. Theirs was a temporary problem. We have nothing to offer such people until they definitely qualify themselves as alcoholics and desire to stop drinking.

9. Those with relatively short alcoholic histories, to whom drinking is more an inconvenience than a matter of life or death.

10. Those who accept only part of the Twelve-Step Program, who will not try to live it in its entirety. Those who wish to place a distorted selfish interpretation on all of the steps for purposes of their own convenience.

11. Those who are psychotic.

Members falling under any of the groups listed, with the possible exception of group 9,

*Read page 70 in the book, "ALCOHOLICS ANONYMOUS."

have little chance of recovery until they see in alcoholism an illness, and are vitally interested in getting well.

Members shown under group 9 need not be unduly alarmed if they are alcoholic and sincerely desire to recover. They can be as successful as any other member. They simply happen to be in a group that has had more difficulty than those in the more advanced stages. Their cue is—to recognize their need for help—have faith—keep open minded.*

Some people reason that although they are not alcoholic, alcoholism could be avoided by belonging to an A.A. group. This is questionable for it is not until the alcoholic has severely punished himself and his family that he gives serious thought to the arresting of his alcoholism. Even then he must prove to himself that he "can't take it." We must pound our heads for a long time against the rough wall of alcoholism before we are convinced.

For those who qualify as real alcoholics and are willing to accept the A.A. program as a means of recovery from alcoholism, we

*Read page 50 in the book, "ALCOHOLICS ANONYMOUS."

recommend a close study of the book, "Alcoholics Anonymous."* *Read it repeatedly.*

This book has all your answers; it was written by alcoholics for alcoholics and is based on the trials and experiences of the first 100 Alcoholics Anonymous members. They worked out a recovery program that has proved to be sound and effective.

By using it as your text book, regularly attending A.A. meetings, and referring to the interpretations of the Twelve Steps as you progress, you will lay a strong foundation upon which *you* can rehabilitate *your* life.

We are not disturbed by the realization that strict adherence to this program demands perfection. We know perfection is impossible. We merely strive toward perfecting ourselves in a way of life that is necessary to bring permanent sobriety, happiness and well-being to real alcoholics.

---

* The book, "ALCOHOLICS ANONYMOUS," is available through your A.A. Group or the Works Publishing, Inc., Grand Central Annex, Box 459, New York 17, N. Y.

Aids to Contented Sobriety

Vital factors contributing to the long records of contented sobriety in the lives of thousands of A.A. members are their *humility, honesty, faith, courage, appreciation* and *service*. The following A.A. definitions will be helpful in working out an acceptable understanding of these vital facts.

Humility

A true evaluation of conditions as they are; willingness to face facts; recognition of our alcoholic status; freedom from false pride and arrogance; understanding of the proper relationship between ourselves and a Higher Power; between ourselves and our fellowman; acceptance of this relationship throughout every 24 hours.

Honesty

Freedom from self-deception; straight-forwardness in our thinking; sincerity in our desire to recover from alcoholism; willingness to admit a wrong; fairness in all our dealings with others.

Faith

Firm in our trust in the A.A. recovery program; belief that we can recover as other members are doing; that practice of the 12 Steps is necessary to happy, contented sobriety; willingness to draw on help from a Higher Power.

COURAGE

A quality of mind which enables us to deal with the problems and realities of life without reliance on alcohol; fortitude to endure the things we cannot change; a determination to stand our ground and "Slug It Out," with all issues, pleasant or otherwise, that might return us to drunkenness; fearlessness in the practice of faith, humility and honesty.

APPRECIATION

Appreciation of the miracle of our sobriety is a healthy state of mind for us to cultivate. As we develop appreciation we enlarge our capacity for happiness, service and contented sobriety. Lack of appreciation and drunkenness are old buddies—they go hand in hand.

SERVICE

Service to God and our fellowmen is the key to A.A. success. Helping other alcoholics who need and want help gives us the tolerance and humility necessary to contented sobriety. Service combats self-centeredness. It reminds us of our own "Powerlessness over Alcohol." It is the life blood of the A.A. fellowship.

The Twelve Steps *

STEP ONE—*Admitted that we were power-less over alcohol and that our lives had become unmanageable.*

STEP TWO—*Came to believe that a Power Greater than Ourselves could restore us to sanity.*

STEP THREE—*Made a decision to turn our will and our lives over to the care of God as we understand Him.*

STEP FOUR—*Made a searching and fearless moral inventory of ourselves.*

STEP FIVE—*Admitted to God, to ourselves and to another human being the exact nature of our wrongs.*

STEP SIX—*We were entirely ready to have God remove all these defects of character.*

STEP SEVEN—*Humbly ask Him to remove our shortcomings.*

* Our Twelve-step Recovery Program is recorded in the book, "ALCOHOLICS ANONYMOUS." See chapters number five, six and seven. The Twelve Steps are to be found on pages seventy-one and seventy-two.

STEP EIGHT—*Made a list of all the people we had harmed and become willing to make amends to them all.*

STEP NINE—*Made direct amends to such people wherever possible, except when to do so would injure them or others.*

STEP TEN—*Continued to take personal inventory and when we were wrong promptly admitted it.*

STEP ELEVEN—*Sought through prayer and meditation to improve our conscious contact with God as we understood Him, praying only for knowledge of His will for us and the power to carry that out.*

STEP TWELVE—*Having had a spiritual experience as the result of these steps, we tried to carry this message to alcoholics, and to practice these principles in all our affairs.*

STEP ONE—*Admitted that we were powerless over alcohol and that our lives had become unmanageable.*

Men and women who are allergic to alcohol and who compulsively persist in its use as a beverage eventually become sick from a unique illness. This illness is known to medicine as alcoholism; it is unique in that it adversely affects one physically, mentally and spiritually.

Step One briefly portrays the pathetic enigma of an uncontrolled drinker who has acquired this illness over which he is entirely powerless.

Drinkers of this type consider alcohol a physical requirement; they gradually increase its consumption at the expense of proper intake of nutritious foods. This practice induces physical and nervous disorders decidedly detrimental to their comfort and health.

The study of Step One concerns the physical illness of alcoholism.*

* The need of truly evaluating our physical condition is emphasized in lines 5-6-12-13-14-15, paragraph two, page two, under "The Doctor's Opinion," in the book, "ALCOHOLICS ANONYMOUS." First read, then study the whole chapter carefully.

Few alcoholics have given their drinking problem much intelligent study. They reluctantly agree they must quit but keep right on drinking.

Severe "hangovers" make them realize that physical illness plays a part in their discomfort but a little "hair off the dog that bit them" is resorted to and they either continue on into a new binge or finally taper off suffering much physical and mental anguish.

The alcoholic lives in compulsive slavery, as alcohol provides the only means he knows by which life is made bearable, or by which he can quiet his jittery nerves. Existence under such circumstances soon makes his life unmanageable.

Correction of this condition is a serious problem of immediate concern. Recovery is possible for alcoholics who honestly want to stop drinking. "Unmanageable lives" and the physical illness induced by compulsive drinking can be arrested. Progress is limited only by our conscious need for help.

The founders of Alcoholics Anonymous identified the physical factor as a part of their "Powerlessness over Alcohol." This "Physical

Factor" was given first consideration in their new "Recovery Program." In twelve simple steps they outlined a *"Way of Life"* for daily practice that restored them to physical health and contented sobriety. Daily practice was their formula for success.

By trial and error they designed a simple philosophy to arrest alcoholism. It embraced knowledge of vital and essential facts. Recovery is possible but a cure cannot be effected. The man or woman who has become an alcoholic cannot become a controlled drinker. They have developed a serious illness against which their lowered physical and mental resistance is powerless. Control over alcohol is gone. Continued drinking now brings only physical illness and insane behavior. They are truly sick people.

Experience has proved that recovery from alcoholism is contingent on:

1. Having a sincere desire to stop drinking.

2. Admitting and believing in our innermost hearts that we are powerless over alcohol.

3. Looking upon alcoholism as a fatal and incurable illness involving the body, mind and spirit.

4. Considering ourselves as patients in A.A. for treatment.

5. Identifying alcohol as a poison rather than a beverage.

6. Making it our business to understand how alcohol affects us.

7. Realizing we are alcoholics.

8. Learning, practicing and having faith in the Twelve Steps of the A.A. program.

9. Believing that we can arrest our alcoholism, but that we can never normally drink again.

10. Gaining a layman's knowledge of alcoholism insofar as it affects our health and well-being.

11. Using this knowledge and understanding of our illness not only to gain sobriety but to guard against the danger of a return to drinking.

12. Doing this partially by keeping in our minds a mental picture of the unmanageable life alcohol demands from us and our powerlessness over it.

The layman's view and understanding of alcoholism is a simple one based on a few facts and backed up with his own experiences plus the knowledge gained from contact with other alcoholics. The following discussion of alcoholism briefly covers the facts necessary to a beginner who will naturally increase his understanding as he makes the Alcoholics Anonymous program his *"Way of Life."*

Nature has provided each normal man and woman with a physical body designed to withstand the rigors of a strenuous daily life.

A healthy person can endure great hardships under most unfavorable circumstances so long as he receives oxygen, water, balanced nutrition, proper rest and relaxation. The human tenacity to retain that "spark of life" is persistent as long as we do not withhold these requisites.

When any one of them are permanently withheld we set up conditions that nature cannot long endure. Sooner or later deficiencies occur in our bodies, nervous tension and neurotic conditions are established; our nervous systems upset mental balance, and we eventually die from lack of rest and nourishment.

Alcoholism stimulates such a condition and

further complicates it by a systematic daily intake of toxic poison—alcohol.

The blood stream and body cells are first affected, then the brain, as we compulsively substitute the poison alcohol for the nutrition necessary to normal health.

This poison irritates the complex organism of the brain and finally breaks down nature's defensive barriers of protection. Physical deterioration is sometimes quite rapid, but in most alcoholics, addiction is acquired over a period of years, so it is only in the later stages of the illness that acute physical breakdown is apparent.

The breakdown is not apparent to the alcoholic. He is unable to visualize the hazardous aspects of his mental or physical condition. Alcoholism has gradually inhibited his power to discern between social and pathological drinking. A marked personality change influenced chiefly by negative thinking now drives the alcoholic to heavier drinking.

Friends and relatives are greatly concerned over this change in personality. But not the alcoholic. His personality precludes self-criticism allowing him but futile adjustment to a normal environment with which he is so much at odds.

Recovery from the illness alcoholism which was responsible for our unmanageable lives can only be accomplished when we stop drinking and return to a permanent, regular, balanced diet that completely eliminates alcohol. *"There is no short cut, no substitute, no other way out for the alcoholic."*

Controlled drinkers have no trouble conforming to this procedure, but the alcoholic who has lowered his physical resistance and exhausted his nervous system should have medical help and care in starting his rehabilitation.

Many members who ignore the importance of their physical well-being as an asset to recovery will fail to arrest their alcoholism. Some may recover but they slow up the process if they do not feel well physically.

We believe that all alcoholics should be hospitalized upon their request for help from Alcoholics Anonymous. This is not presently possible in all cases so the members who cannot receive hospital care are cautioned to consult a competent doctor who is skilled in the diagnosis and treatment of alcoholism.

The importance of this advice cannot be over emphasized. The alcoholic is a sick man. He does not realize it and wishes to minimize his physical condition. This should not be allowed by the older members; they should point out the need of a complete physical check-up and see that the new member gets it.

Those who neglect the simple precaution of receiving ethical medical care are less apt to effect a speedy recovery from alcoholism.

The alcoholic, whose life has become unmanageable from uncontrolled drinking, is taking a serious step when he identifies himself with our program and attempts to make it his "Way of Life." His future security depends on the successful attainment of A.A. as a "Way of Life." He cannot allow impaired physical well being to detract from his chances of recovery; therefore he must safeguard his health, as poor health may return him to drinking.

The new member will do well to investigate the various phases of alcoholism that apply to his case; he should admit that he is an alcoholic and discuss his problems with older members who are always willing to offer advice and render help.

Learn to see in alcoholism a diseased condition of the nervous system due to the excessive use of alcohol. Reflect upon your powerlessness over this sickness. Learn a number of the tests in the medical and psychological field that identify alcoholics. Admit that you "can't take it." Consider your inability to "take it or leave it alone;" remember that your inability to leave it alone, in the face of impending disaster if you take it, definitely marks you as an alcoholic. The necessity of a drink "the morning after" is common to most alcoholics. There are many other identifications of the alcoholic —make it your business to learn some of them.

The founders of Alcoholics Anonymous understood that the member would have to realize his physical illness and receive medical help before he could fully employ his mental faculties on the spiritual requirements necessary to our program. Physical health is a neccessity but only a first step in recovery from our alcoholic illness.

SUMMARIZATION — Recovery from alcoholism first involves a layman's knowledge of our illness and a conscious need for its treatment. There is no mystery about it. Addiction to alcohol has set up a toxic poisoning within our physical bodies. Compulsive drinking, over which we are powerless, naturally follows. "Our lives become unmanageable." The first step of recovery is to recognize our alcoholism and admit our physical illness.

WHY DOES THIS HELP? It makes us honest in evaluating our true physical condition. It makes us humble and willing to stop alcoholic rationalization. It awakens us to our need for hospitalization before entering A.A. and for competent medical care afterwards.

WHY ARE WE SICK? CAN WE BE CURED? Real alcoholics are sick from toxic poisoning acquired by substituting alcohol for food and rest. Physical health can be restored but no cure will permit us to become controlled drinkers.

Treatment. Admitting our alcoholism. Willingness to accept medical treatment. Personal effort to supplement medical care with proper diet and relaxation. Belief we can recover. Daily practice of our A.A. program.

DRUGS

Occasionally, some of us have resorted to drugs to give physical comfort or to induce sleep. This practice is *out* for all alcoholics, except those rare cases where an ethical medical practitioner, skilled in the treatment of alcoholism, prescribes and supervises such treatment.

We live the A.A. program to develop normal, well-integrated personalities that exclude the use of the narcotic alcohol. Drugs prevent this change in personality. They warp our thinking. They too quickly become a substitute for alcohol and are decidedly habit forming for most of us.

By drugs we mean bromides, chlorhydrate, paraldehyde, all barbiturates (Goof Balls), opiates and benzedrine. We know from experience the unsatisfactory record of A.A. members who continue willfully to use them. We know that these drugs change our mental processes. They prevent honesty and realism. Our 24-hour program of A.A. living demands *Faith* in a *Power Greater than Ourselves* so we must surrender self-will and entirely eliminate the use of these drugs.

STEP TWO—*Came to believe that a Power Greater than Ourselves could restore us to sanity.* *

The purpose of this step is to disclose the nature of the mental illness which we have suffered from alcoholism and to believe that we can overcome it by help from a *Power Greater than Ourselves.*

No real alcoholic acts sanely while drinking. Chronic poisoning from alcohol results in compulsive drinking and insane behavior. Will power is not a factor in recovery until the compulsion has been removed. Since reservations defeat any honest attempt to stop drinking, we find it necessary to recognize our mental disability. Dodging the truth only results in distorted thinking and opposition to help from a *Power Greater than Ourselves.*

Those of us who have had an honest desire to recover from the mental sickness that alcoholism has imposed upon us have successfully used this *Power.* Our sick personalities find a sure source of power and healing in *God as We Understand Him.* God renews our minds and straightens out our thinking.

* Before reading this chapter consult pages **48, 49, and 50** in the book, "ALCOHOLICS ANONYMOUS."

What you call this *Power* is a matter of your own choice. Call It what you will. Its recovery value lies in the fact you believe It exists, that you approach It with faith and that you sincerely depend upon It to restore you to mental fitness.

Harmony with God is the only hope of the alcoholic; it is possible by making A.A. your way of life. The acceptance and practice of the Twelve Steps of the A.A. program will give you a conscious contact with this *Power Greater than Yourself*; it will restore you to sane thinking.

The inability of the uncontrolled drinker to be self critical often causes him to waste time in useless discussion of the use of the word sanity in Step Two. He is willing to concede his physical and spiritual illness but objects to any question of his mental soundness. We offer the following explanation for members with such opinions.

The beginner will avoid confusion in his interpretation of this step if he approaches it with a sincere desire for the accepted A.A. meaning. Remind yourself that you are making the A.A. recovery program your way of life because it is essential to your recovery from alcoholism. On it depends the well-being of your mind and body, your happiness and the security of your home—your very life. It might very well be suicide to disagree with any part of it, so resolve to be open-minded and accept the Twelve Steps in their entirety.

Some members have eventually arrived at the true meaning of Step Two by temporarily rephrasing it to read, "Came to believe that a *Power Greater than Ourselves* could restore us to sane behavior."

The truth of the matter is that most of our members have only acted on the level of insanity during periods of intoxication. This is common practice to all drinkers who get "tight," but to the alcoholic who shortens the intervals between his periods of intoxication and finally merges them into one long "drunk," it becomes a serious matter. Insane behavior because of an evening's drinking is generally excused, but when carried on for weeks and months that lengthen into years, it becomes a fixed pattern that is sponsored by the brain.

We cannot overlook the harmful effect of the prolonged use of alcohol on the brain or that it does produce an unhealthy mental condition which results in a complacent disregard of sane thought or normal behavior. The alcoholic cannot control his impulses; he lacks mental coordination. Continued use of alcohol damages the brain and in some cases brings on insanity.

Various degrees of brain injury exist in all alcoholics in proportion to their physical resistance to alcohol poisoning and to the length of time involved in abnormal drinking.

The alcoholic who wishes to cling to the illusion that he exercises sanity in his drinking is invited to prove his case against the accepted definition of insanity.

A simple definition of insanity is a disorder of behavior that occurs when the body impulses no longer find in the brain a coordinating center for the conditioning of behavior. When this condition arises man's behavior is unpredictable and he becomes legally insane.

The behavior of the uncontrolled drinker who has become alcoholic is likewise unpredictable and his friends and relatives take on a long face as alcoholism perverts his power of reason, dulls his talent, limits his instinct of self preservation, makes him irresponsible, and adversely affects his behavior.

How is the alcoholic to account for that insane impulse which prompts him to reach for the *First Drink* that starts him off on another "binge?"

Is it a sane act? Is he obsessed? Is it the result of an urge which is sponsored by irrational thinking? Does it involve thinking?

Does sanity in an alcoholic imply his power to accept or reject that *First Drink?*

We think it does as we do not believe that he can help himself. We believe and know from experience that a *Power Greater than Himself* can remove his obsession, straighten out his thinking, and restore him to sane thought and behavior.

Those who disapprove the use of the word sanity in Step Two are usually alcoholics who have been fortunate enough to escape the more serious aspects of alcoholism. They reason that they were perfectly normal between drinking bouts.*

The alcoholic who did himself no serious

* Read pages 32, 33, and 34 in the book, "ALCOHOLICS ANONYMOUS."

40

damage during his drinking career should find solace in that fact. He should take a broad view of the insanity of alcoholism, however, as most of us were surely deranged over varying periods of time.

He must also remember that in the progressive development of alcoholism the power of reasoning is slowly deteriorated. This encourages deception as to our real mental health and fitness; it breeds a superior feeling of false security.

Evidence to support this fact is found in the following danger symptoms commonly seen in alcoholics:

1. Taking that *First Drink* with the idea that *This Time I'll Control It.*

2. The continued use of alcohol and reliance upon it for physical and mental power to meet our daily responsibilities.

3. The necessity of the drink "the morning after."

4. Our inability to be self-critical of the sanity of our behavior over prolonged years of drinking—our refusal to consider the harm we have done to ourselves and others.

5. The faith we placed in childish excuses for our drinking and the stupid alibis we thought we were getting away with.

6. The reckless abandon we displayed in drunken driving—the argument that we drive better drunk than sober and our resentment toward those who differed from this opinion.

7. The critical physical condition we reach and the continued suffering we endure from uncontrolled drinking.

8. The financial risks taken—the shame, sorrow and often poverty that we inflict upon our families.

9. The asinine resentments that clogged our minds—our loss of responsibility—getting ourselves drunk to spite or injure others—the erroneous assumption that we can "take it or leave it alone"—our unnecessary squandering of money.

10. "Black outs."

11. Contemplated or attempted suicide.

These are a few symptoms, common to alcoholics, indicating mental illness. They justify our deduction that alcohol, in large or small doses, has become a poison that induces unpredictable behavior and limits mental coordination.

There is no point in deceiving ourselves regarding the fate of the alcoholic, the uncontrolled drinker, if he continues to use alcohol. He has just two escapes from drinking, one is insanity; the other is alcoholic death. The purpose of the A.A. program as a *"Way of Life"* is to avoid both by arresting the illness alcoholism.

As alcoholics we cannot undo our past behavior; we can, however, use the knowledge of our escape from insanity and alcoholic death as an incentive to contact God for help in keeping us from future drinking.

It is now our privilege to draw on the help of a *Power Greater than Ourselves* to arrest our alcoholism. The alcoholic record of our past life is not the basis upon which our future will be judged. We have a new page before us; we are invited to "write our own ticket." Sobriety, sanity, security and peace of mind are within our reach.

The future, with the A.A. program as *"Our Way of Life,"* will bring us sane, useful, happy lives. We have learned our lesson; namely, that for us alcohol is poison that brings mental illness and insane behavior.

Surely, with this knowledge, we can never lay claim to sanity if we again take that First Drink.

MENTAL DRUNKENNESS

In spite of all this knowledge some of us willfully continue in self-centeredness. We ignore our mental illness. Alcoholic thinking displaces humility and we return to physical drunkenness through lack of spiritual strength and understanding.

Checking the reasons for our failure we discover that over a period of time we have built up resentment, self-pity, physical or mental exhaustion and that our faith in a *Power Greater than Ourselves* was inadequate.

We should never forget that our physical drunks are always preceded by mental binges that end in spiritual blackouts. They leave us blind and helpless, insulating us from the "Power" upon which our sanity and sobriety depends. We can detect them if we will observe the danger signals so apparent during the buildup of the mental binge.

SUMMARIZATION—Mental illness. Variable degrees of mental illness precede the ultimate end of all alcoholics who persist in drinking. The practice of Step Two shows us how to avoid the ultimate end of all drinking alcoholics: Insanity or alcoholic death.

Symptoms of the Mental Illness of Alcoholism. Rebelling against our alcoholic illness, rationalizing that first drink, self-pity, condemnation of others, inability to be self-critical, resentment, "stinking thinking," mental drunkenness, emotional instability ("self-will run riot"), blackouts, contemplated suicide, attempted suicide, delusions, hallucinations, delirium tremens.

Treatment. 1. Honest evaluation of our sick personalities and of the inadequacy of the human will to remedy them. 2. Conscious need for treatment. 3. Willingness to receive proper treatment. 4. Belief that *A Power Greater than Ourselves* can restore us to sane thought and behavior. 5. Dependence upon a Higher Power for recovery from our mental illness.

Recovery. We attain spiritual strength, understanding, humility, emotional stability, peace of mind and contented sobriety.

STEP THREE—*Made a decision to turn our will and our lives over to the care of God as we understand Him.*

The objective of the study of Steps One, Two and Three is to identify alcoholism as a three-fold illness that has made inroads upon our physical health, our mental well being and our spiritual status.

A complete knowledge of the injury we have suffered at the hands of "John Barleycorn" is indispensable to our recovery from alcoholism.

The purpose of Step Three is to recognize and treat a malady none of us formerly looked upon as a sickness, this malady is spiritual illness. A.A., as a *"Way of Life,"* is basically a spiritual program that arrests alcoholism as we develop within ourselves a true sense of responsibility to God and to our fellow men.

Knowledge and treatment of our physical and mental sickness are vital necessities, but lasting sobriety is maintained only by daily treatment of our spiritual illness.

As uncontrolled drinkers we have lived our lives willfully and selfishly bringing unhappiness, trouble and disgrace upon ourselves. Our powerlessness over alcohol outweighed the regard we held for our own security or our good intentions toward our loved ones.

The remorse that drinking brought filled us with kindly intent toward deserving friends and relatives, but never allowed us to make permanent restitution. Resolutions and good intentions bolstered great faith within us during periods of sobriety, but being spiritually ill, we were unable to carry out our plans. Our "dog house" existence was occasionally relieved by sane and thoughtful acts during sober moments only to be resumed upon the next drunk, until we lost faith in ourselves. We were strong willed in all matters except in our ability to control our drinking, our drinking behavior, or our treatment of others.

It is not until we are fully aware of these facts that we become "fed up" with our inability to assume or execute normal responsibilities. It is only when we realize and admit the fact that "Our troubles were self imposed and that we were extreme examples of self will run riot" that we are ready to look outside ourselves for help.

Alcoholics who have accepted and practiced Step Three know the value of turning their will and their lives over to the care of God as they understand Him. Faith in the power of God, as they understand Him, has brought them happiness and sobriety as it promoted recovery from the spiritual illness of alcoholism.

Some of us hesitated to face the requirements of this step for fear of public opinion or because it seemed hypocritical to turn to God for help after ignoring Him for years.

It is well to realize that we belong to an anonymous society; that the public has no way of knowing what we are doing *except that we no longer drink.* The fact is that although they did not accept us while we drank, they honor and receive us when we stop.

We were unable to stop of our own volition; we tried devious ways of controlling our drinking and to regulate our lives; we did everything within our power and knowledge to escape the effects of alcoholism.

The sensible thing to do now, if we are serious about gaining permanent sobriety, is to surrender our false pride, as thousands of other alcoholics have done, and effect our recovery from alcoholism under the care of *God as We Understand Him.* The fact that thousands of alcoholics have recovered and that new hundreds are daily doing it by help from a *Power Greater than Ourselves* should leave no doubt about our chances of recovery.*

Those of us who claim it hypocritical to now turn to God and ask for help because of alcoholic problems are still avoiding responsibility. We know what should be done about the matter but are not being honest with ourselves when we refuse to accept His help. Our reasoning is still along the line of escape from reality; we are still dealing in the alibi of the alcoholic.

This sort of reasoning will continue our insane behavior and spiritual illness as it leads us back to drunkenness. We must accept the need and authenticity of each step in the Alcoholics Anonymous program if we are to make it our *"Way of Life."*

There is no provision in any of the Twelve Steps that justifies the questioning of God's willingness to extend help for our recovery,

*Read pages 59 and 60 in the book, "ALCOHOLICS ANONYMOUS."

providing we are sincere in our determination to get well.

Fear, pride, resentment, egotism, willfulness and all the undesirable traits that make up the personality of the alcoholic should be submitted to the care of God for supervision and constructive reconditioning.

Forgetting the seemingly overwhelming importance of our alcoholic problems, we must learn to rely on His power. Self-will becomes less difficult to renounce when we consider the part it has played in "messing up our lives."

Think for a minute of the futility of self-centered alcoholic living; recall the emptiness and suffering of alcoholic-inspired self-exaltation; remember the defeat and despair it brought us, the ill health, the irrational thinking and the insane behavior.

We must agree that any will, other than our own, could have regulated our affairs to better advantage. Surely we have been kidding ourselves long enough. It is time to take on an understanding of God's will and make ourselves a channel for its expression.

We have before us the examples of A.A.

members who are doing their best to learn the meaning of God's will and to constantly draw on His power for help. It is interesting to note that these members have exchanged their old alcoholic personalities for the sane happy personality of the sincere A.A. member.

Honesty, humility and willingness to establish an alert consciousness of this *Power Greater than Ourselves* is the first requirement in trying to understand God.

Success in improving our conscious contact with God results from faith in His power, from meditation, from prayer, from observation of members whom you feel have made a contact with Him, from discussion of Step Three with such members.*

We get nowhere trying to force a contact or understanding. It must come naturally as we surrender our problems to Him. We gain an understanding of this matter as we unselfishly go about the business of understanding another fellow's problem and trying to help him. God often shows us the answer to our own problem through solution of the other fellow's

*Understanding God is complicated by our useless analysis of Him. Spiritual awakening springs from daily "Practice of His Presence."

difficulties. The faith we practice with relaxed patience, as we work out the Twelve Steps of the A.A. program, assures us an understanding of this *Power Greater than Ourselves.*

The new member should not confuse any part of the Alcoholics Anonymous philosophy with his church or organized religion. Keep your religion but do not substitute it for A.A. Honest clergymen expedite spiritual attainment yet lack understanding of the physical and mental ills of alcoholism.

Religious views are things to be dealt with outside of A.A. Your conception of *God as You Understand Him,* the fact that you believe in a *Power Greater than Yourself* to restore you to spiritual health, is all that our program requires.

"As soon as a man says he does believe or is willing to believe, we emphatically assure him that he is on his way.

"It has been repeatedly proved among us that upon this simple cornerstone a wonderful effective spiritual structure can be built."*

*Read page 59 in the book, "ALCOHOLICS ANONYMOUS."

Belief and faith in God are necessary to the alcoholic; in them he finds the solution of a happy sober life. They bring him peace of mind, an active useful life, strength and understanding to combat his daily problems, the power to resist alcohol, the ability to develop mental and spiritual health, the opportunity to amend his past errors.

Few newcomers need any introduction to the idea of a *Divine Being*. Most of us were taught this in our youth. We have all seen evidence of a *Power Greater than Ourselves* in our well-regulated world of fixed seasons, of day and night, of heat and moisture; peopled by the reproduction of human life and made livable by love and tolerance of human beings.

Most of us have studied the perfection of the universe, the animation of living things, the action of the human mind, the power of love. These things all seem to denote a dynamic Life Force that is back of, in and through everything about us. This force appears to direct all things harmoniously but irresistibly toward a natural, definite, useful conclusion.

Is it hard to recognize in this Life Force

a *Power Greater than Ourselves?* Do we not feel Its creative energy and sense, intelligence and power that makes man most insignificant by comparison?

Does he not remain insignificant as long as he ignores the *Power?* Experience shows that he becomes a source of constructive energy when he identifies himself with It and makes himself an agent for Its fulfillment.

We identify ourselves with this Life Force, this *Power Greater than Ourselves,* when we:

1. Assume an attitude of surrender of self-centered interests.

2. Assume a humble attitude of faith backed by a sincere desire for sobriety.

3. Assume the willingness to pray unselfishly.

4. Assume and believe that we are spiritually ill.

5. Assume the responsibility of overcoming our illness.

6. Make a decision to place our will and life in God's care for treatment.

7. Pray without resentment in our hearts.

8. Do the positive things that eliminate our defects of character.

9. Sense the necessity of cleanliness of heart.

10. Become forgiving of others.

11. Recognize the spiritual potentialities within us.

12. Try to understand God with a view toward developing these potentialities.

The important thing is our willingness to *try*. Every man and woman has spiritual possibilities. We must learn to bring them out, to form convictions and let them grow.

When it is possible we should take our wives or close relatives into our confidence as we attempt to carry out this step. We have found that there is great strength and help to the member who has the confidence and cooperation of those close to him. If they are not cooperative he must work it out alone.

We should avoid the common mistake of confusing our minds with anxious thoughts regarding the time and manner God will manifest Himself to us. Our understanding will come gradually as we earn and develop it.

It is uncommon for a member to have a drastic spiritual upheaval. Spiritual awakening or experience comes slowly and often in strange ways. It does come, however, but so naturally that we many times fail to recognize it.

Our job is to be ready and willing for these experiences, to take an incentive from the example of fellow members who are living the A.A. program, to be open-minded in our endeavor to understand God, to realize that it is not made up of one big accomplishment but is gained bit by bit, and that our inspiration will be influenced by our attitude and action.* The active member who takes the program seriously by applying it to his home life, in his business, in the treatment of new members, by admitting wrongs and by making amends is establishing a way, both mental and physical, for a close personal contact with God.

Quiet periods of relaxation and prayer are most necessary to the achievement of this step. The alcoholic should also keep in mind the value of relaxation aside from prayer. We

* Our recovery from alcoholism seems to be dependent on appreciation of and thankfulness for the help from a Higher Power.

should not overlook the fact that all alcoholics are of restless disposition, that restlessness and tension are a part of our trouble, that we once appeased this condition with alcohol, that we now seek to correct it under Divine supervision.

The alcoholic must learn to "let go" whenever he becomes upset, when over-activity brings him feelings of mental and physical exhaustion, when he becomes extremely impatient, when he experiences anger, when he is bored, when he is resentful.

Relaxation helps us maintain physical, mental and spiritual balance. It aids clear thinking that keeps us out of the "Driver's Seat." It permits "Conscious Contact with God"— our only hope for recovery from alcoholism.

We regard the outcome of this step in complete confidence, as we know from the example of other members that God's will can be understood, that our understanding of His care will give us new personalities that exclude alcohol—personalities that do happily relate us to God, to a conventional world, and to our fellow men.

SUMMARIZATION—The confusing ills of alcoholism need no longer frustrate the alcoholic
who wants to get well. A.A. clearly reveals
alcoholism as a "Sickness"—a fatal, incurable malady.

Chronic alcoholic poisoning induced by addiction to alcohol accounts for our physical
and mental illness. This illness is the premise
upon which we base our "Decision" to seek
God's help for recovery.

Spiritual illness loses its mystery and vague-
ness when we concede the anesthetic role alcohol has played in our lives. It explains the
mental paralysis and moral deviations asso-
ciated with compulsive drinking. We come to
know that self-pity, fear, intolerance, resentment, belligerency, vindictiveness and dishonesty have insulated us from God. They have
calloused our consciences. They have bred
spiritual illness.

Treatment. We stop playing God. We surrender our self-centeredness to Him. We relax.
We avoid confusing A.A. with religion. We do
not try to define God. We recognize and attempt to develop our spiritual possibilities. We
seek a personal contact with God practicing

faith, tolerance, forgiveness, honesty, meditation and unselfish prayer in our approach to Him as the means of recovering from alcoholism.

STEP FOUR—*Made a searching and fearless moral inventory of ourselves.*

The purpose of taking a moral inventory is to expose the noxious character traits of our alcoholic personalities, to eliminate them from the new personalities that with the help of the Alcoholics Anonymous Program as a *"Way of Life,"* we now propose to develop.

The A.A. usage of the term "personality" deals with the development of new character traits necessary to our recovery from alcoholism. It has no relation to personal magnetism emanating from physical health, beauty or charm.

We gauge A.A. personality by A.A. maturity that is evidenced in such qualities as: Strength and understanding from a *Power Greater than Ourselves,* surrender of self-centeredness, honesty, sincerity, practice of the Twelve Steps, creative thoughts, positive action in admitting wrongs and making amends, service to others and the example of a happy sober life.

Before we can hope to develop the qualities that will create desirable A.A. personalities, we must discover the causes for our powerlessness over alcohol; we wish to know why we have been at war with ourselves; we propose to reveal and to study the limitations that alcoholism has placed upon our lives.

We hope to transcend our alcoholic limitations, to straighten out our unmanageable lives so we check our alcoholic personalities, "To search out the flaws in our make-up which caused our failure."*

The gravity of our drinking problem is deep-seated; it involves self-centered habits, emotions, moods, attitudes, and misconceptions acquired over a period of years. They have decreased our mental powers, weakened our physical resistance, and have sponsored irrational thought and action. This has caused us extreme mental and physical hardship and brought anxiety and suffering to others.

Arresting our alcoholism is not possible until we have a knowledge of our defects, therefore, we take definite steps toward correction of our physical, mental, and spiritual disability when we make a searching and fearless moral inventory of ourselves; when we do it in

*Read page 76 in the book, "ALCOHOLICS ANONYMOUS."

a thorough businesslike way; when we reasonably excuse the other fellow and truly expose
our own faults.

The beginner cannot fail to be impressed
with the array of flaws he will uncover and
will wish to correct. The caution to be observed in taking this step is that *Few of Us Are
Ready and Willing to Surrender All of Our
Defects*. We wish to cherish a few and by this
procedure we encounter future trouble in the
form of partial rehabilitation which is not the
plan of the A.A. recovery program.

This step calls for a *complete inventory;*
our program is not in accord with halfway
measures or efforts; full rehabilitation is our
objective. Reservations defeat this purpose.
They take the soberness out of sobriety. Let's
be wise and employ the inventory one hundred
percent.

A moral inventory of a lifetime of drinking
is not quickly recorded, nor is it a record that
can be simply stated. We find in it many complexities that require study and meditation. It
must be honest, sincere, and thorough. To be
effective it must be a written inventory as it
will later be checked against and often re-

ferred to. The mental self-appraisal is merely a supplement to the written inventory. It is necessary but not sufficient in itself.

Experience has taught us that this step should be started at once, but left open for future reference so that during the process of our mental and spiritual clean-up we can add the new items that will present themselves.

The brief discussion of a few imperfections permitted in this book is entirely inadequate to the thought and time you will need in applying this step to your alcoholic problem.

Reference to pages 76 to 83 inclusive in the Alcoholics Anonymous Book will disclose a detailed discussion of Step Four. From these pages you will learn the manner in which our founders advocate that we work out our inventories.

You will discover that various manifestations of self-centeredness are undoubtedly the root of our trouble and that some of these manifestations present themselves in the form of Resentment — Dishonesty — Self-pity — Jealousy — Criticism — Intolerance — Fear — Anger.

RESENTMENT

Resentment is common to all alcoholics. We are never safe from it and as intangible as it may seem, it does pay off in material ways with destructive force and energy. Resentment is dynamite to the alcoholic.

In studying the book, "Alcoholics Anonymous," we are reminded that "resentment is the *Number One Offender*." It destroys more alcoholics than anything else. From it stems all forms of spiritual disease, for we have not only been mentally and physically ill, we have been spiritually sick. When the spiritual malady is overcome, we straighten out mentally and physically.

"In dealing with resentments we set them on paper. We list people, institutions and principles with whom we were angry. We ask ourselves why we were angry. In most cases we found that our self-esteem, our pocketbooks, our relationships (including sex), our ambitions were hurt or threatened. So we were sore; we were burnt up."*

Make up your grudge list; see whom you are enclosing in your circle of hatred; determine why you hold them there. Has your life

*Study pages 76-77, book, "ALCOHOLICS ANONYMOUS."

been any happier because of this resentment? Were they really the offenders?

The founders of Alcoholics Anonymous answer the question with the definite statement: "It is plain that a life which includes deep resentments leads only to futility and unhappiness. To the precise extent that we permit these, do we squander the hours that might have been worth while."

They explain that resentment dwarfs the maintenance and growth of spiritual experience which is the only hope of the alcoholic and that without the sunlight of this experience the insanity of alcoholism returns and we drink again.

DISHONESTY

"Those who do not recover through the help of our program are usually men and women who will not give themselves to the program and who are constitutionally incapable of being honest with themselves."

Dishonesty requires little further comment. It has no place in our program. It must be eliminated if we are to succeed at all.

Honesty with yourself, God, and your fellow man is the keystone in the A.A. bridge that spans the alcoholic chasm to permanent happy sobriety.

Without honesty the A.A. program would become an inconsistent, hypocritical way of life. It would become negative and cease to be constructive. The practice of dishonesty in any form helps to tear down the alcoholics defense against that first drink which he will eventually find himself taking, if he cannot be honest with himself.

CRITICISM

Criticism, a form of negative judgment, is absolutely out of our fellowship picture. It is a black sheep in the A.A. family; a malicious carrier of strife and rebellion. It deprives us of peace of mind and contented sobriety.

Well-meant advice that is solicited can be most helpful and is encouraged because of its sincerity; but not criticism.

It is viciously opposed to the A.A. personalities we are trying to develop. It is not a gesture of cooperation indicating friendly interest but rather a destructive force that breeds self-pity, jealousy and resentment.

The Common Interest of the A.A. Program Is Sobriety. Criticism has no place in helping either an individual or a group to gain or maintain SOBRIETY.

Fault-finding and gossip will destroy the results of much constructive A.A. effort. They serve no good purpose so should be controlled with tolerance and understanding, thus curbing our tendencies toward criticism.

If you must deal in criticism, confine your practice to self-criticism.

SELF-PITY

Self-pity is not generally regarded by alcoholics as a particularly harmful emotion. We have all indulged in varied forms of self-pity, the most common being the type experienced while enduring the tortures of a hangover. Other forms of self-pity involve resentment and hatred brought on by real or fancied wrongs, by acts of God, by ill luck or disease.

Self-pity is often outright rebellion against circumstances of our own making where we feel sorry for ourselves and assume a negative attitude toward life.

It is not until we see in this emotion evidence of resentment and until we realize that it gives us the wrong attitude toward life and toward those with whom we associate, that we understand the necessity for its elimination.

The alcoholic must free himself from all forms of resentment; his happiness in life depends on his attitude and service toward others. He cannot afford to subject himself to self-pity because of its relationship to resentment and inferiority. It also retards his recovery from alcoholism by closing his mind to the wholesome helpful opportunities about him; it promotes self-centered thinking that should be directed toward understanding God and establishing an intimate relationship with Him.

Emotional maturity and A.A. growth are stunted by self-pity. This extreme form of self-centeredness lacks faith and stunts spiritual growth. We seek God's help to treat this most serious character defect.

Treatment. Recognize self-pity. Pray to lose this defect. Cultivate appreciation of your sobriety. Thank God for it. Help another alcoholic. Thus we develop new spiritual strength that surplants fear and dependency. Thus we eliminate Self-pity.

JEALOUSY

Few, if any, men or women escape this emotional monstrosity. Its width and length are fear and suspicion. Its depth is anger and frustration.

Jealousy of an individual's good standing, his personality, his talent or personal possessions can prey upon the human mind until, like a malignant cancer, it injures or destroys.

The beginner who takes the time to analyze jealousy finds in it a combination of all his pet imperfections. You are advised to make this analysis and thus acquaint yourself with its negative character.

Search it for "Blind Spots" that lead alcoholics back to compulsive drinking.

A close inspection will show an astounding array of moral defects. They may appear in mild or passive form, yet they are all there: Self-pity — Resentment — Intolerance — Dishonesty — Criticism — Suspicion — Anger. From this inspection we learn that fear and frustration bind them all together.

It is well to avoid this compound emotion

which can so easily jeopardize a member's mental health and lead him into resentment, bitter hatred and drunkenness.

INTOLERANCE

Lack of tolerance has much to do with that first drink which under certain circumstances the alcoholic is unable to resist.

This condition existed when physical distress was experienced, when the realities of life became too demanding on our time and energy; when mental tension was great, when resentment at home or in business became unbearable, when business was poor, when we became fatigued through over-activity or we were faced with other distracting circumstances. We felt that conditions had reached a breaking point; we became intolerant of them, so we got drunk.

We should never forget the intolerable hangovers and the despair of compulsive drinking; or God's help in its removal. We need more help with new problems. Do not expect God to eliminate them overnight. The practice of tolerance is a part of recovery.

It aids spiritual progress and improves emotional stability. It nurtures contented sobriety.

Evidence of intolerance in a member is not a good sign. It shows lack of equilibrium and indicates symptoms of an unstable mental and spiritual status. Our attitude of tolerance, where it should reasonably be expected, reflects our understanding and practice of the A.A. philosophy as a *"Way of Life."*

The alcoholic has consistently poached on the tolerance of mankind. He has much to amend in this respect, and should reverse his field at once by showing consideration where it is due.

We do not believe that tolerance of improper situations makes good sense. God gave us intelligence to determine between good and bad, therefore, we find as much harm in being tolerant of wrong thought or action as we find in intolerance of the right things.

Discretion in the use of tolerance is necessary, but if we are practicing the A.A. program as a *"Way of Life,"* we will find ourselves meeting halfway, those people of whom we have long been intolerant. Tolerance toward both new and old members who are sincerely trying to live this program is essential to our own recovery from alcoholism. If they are honestly trying to make A.A. their *"Way of Life,"* we owe them our help.

It is not wise to become intolerant of conditions that you cannot change; the A.A. program advises you to gain an understanding of God's will. The condition that cannot be changed may be against the will of God. You should not view it with intolerance, but rather direct your time and energy in helpful constructive activity where satisfactory results are possible.

"God grant us the serenity to accept the things we cannot change, courage to change the things we can, and wisdom to know the difference."

FEAR

The tendency of alcoholics to discount fear as contributing to alcoholism often causes newcomers to underrate its importance to their inventories. They erroneously associate fear with cowardice and want no part of it. Yet fear had much to do with their drinking and full knowledge of it is essential to their recovery.

It is an emotion that has a definite place in the lives of all human beings. Primitive man could not have survived without it. Experience made him afraid of dangerous or destructive things against which he was powerless and fear then supplied the extra energy needed to avoid or escape them.

When used for actual purposes of self-preservation, fear gives us the caution and the discretion necessary to the requirements of every day living. Fear prompts us to take safe procedures and to protect our families against poverty and disease. Under its impulse we gain energy to build homes; to work; to face reality, and to assume responsibility.

As alcoholics we have used a few of fears positive qualities but utilized mostly the negative ones, specializing to a great extent on anxiety, dread, worry, uncertainty, and apprehension of harm or evil that always seemed just around the corner. Urged by fear of hangovers and alcoholic insomnia we hid liquor all over our homes. Fear of truth filled us with dread and uncertainty. Anxiety constantly beset our effort to conceal addiction, to uphold our lies, to dodge our creditors.

Fear of domination, public opinion, loss of home and finances allowed no peace of mind.

The negative elements of fear belong in our inventories. Reference to pages 77 and 78 of the A.A. Book will disclose examples of fear in our lives and outline a way of classification. Part of our personality change centers around our understanding and treatment of this emotion.

The A.A. program is not founded upon fear. It is a spiritual *Way of Life* based on *Power* other than our own, on faith in a *Power Greater than Ourselves* to overcome fear and other defects of our alcoholic personalities. We have seen members try to find contented sobriety basing their attempt on self-education motivated by the fear of alcohol. They do not stay sober long. We have known them to try to protect themselves from drinking by total absence from bars and night clubs under the assumption that they would be sorely tempted by such environment. From their experience we believe that such abnormal worry indicates a half-hearted attempt at the program and is in reality an unacknowledged desire to drink again.

Page 113 of the A.A. Book advises us, "In

our belief any scheme of combating alcoholism which proposes to shield the sick man from temptation is doomed to failure. If the alcoholic tries to shield himself, he may succeed for a time, but usually winds up with a bigger explosion than ever. We have tried these methods. These attempts to do the impossible have failed. So our rule is not to avoid a place where there is drinking *if we have a legitimate reason for being there*. Go or stay away, whatever seems best. But be sure you are on solid spiritual ground before you start and that your motive in going is thoroughly good."

Being on spiritual ground is the important thing but we must not overlook the fact that we have a definite part to play. God can help us only if we are willing and trying to get well. Realization that temptation will always be present and that we never have successfully avoided it before should bring us close to God for help. We have no knowledge of how or when the urge to drink will come. We know that it will, however, and that we cannot wait until it is upon us. We must prepare ourselves with faith in the program and meditation and prayer with God.

Steps Numbers One and Two can be most helpful in reminding us why we must submit our fear to God. We are never to forget our powerlessness over alcohol and the insane behavior and unmanageable living it brings. Nature backs up this theory with drunken dreams. Dreams that are so realistic they fill us with genuine remorse and further our determination to gain contented sobriety.

We must admit that we are alcoholic, it is good for us to do so. All members should strive to cultivate an honest realistic evaluation of what alcohol does to them as partial insurance against a possible return to drinking. This does not imply the use of fear but rather of intelligence to avoid further alcohol addiction. We are not afraid of alcohol. Alcohol can be all around us without harmful effect if our "spiritual ground" is right and we are on a 24-hour practice of our philosophy. We should, however, be afraid to drink it, just as afraid of it as any other poison.

Thus we fortify our minds with prayer and with the mental resources God has given us. Intelligent use of mental portraits, based on knowledge of our alcoholic status, are invaluable to our recovery from alcoholism. We do not rebel against the fact we cannot drink or use poisons generally. Contented sobriety will come easier when we have learned to take alcohol out of the beverage classification and place it where it rightfully belongs for us— among the poisons.

Members who are unable to overcome their fear by practice of the A.A. program should consult their doctor or psychiatrist who will probably be able to help them. Such aid plus help from our program usually straightens them out and makes sobriety possible.

Fear that does not constitute an obsession can be corrected by the philosophy provided in our A.A. program. Fear is nothing more or less than a distorted faith in the negative things of life and the evils *that might beset us.*

A.A. philosophy does not concern itself with anxiety or fear. As alcoholics we were once unstable because of problems and anxieties that seemed impossible to remedy. The spiritual concepts of this program have removed them and have replaced them with peace of mind. We no longer worry; we have received a spiritual reprieve. This reprieve is extended from day to day by God in recognition of our appreciation of His help and the unselfish service we render to others.

Our antidote for fear is faith, not the distorted faith in fear, but rehabilitating all out faith in God as we understand Him. We have found this to be an effective measure in overcoming all fears the alcoholic is subjected to.

ANGER

There is no single instance covered in the Twelve Steps where anger offers any benefit. We are led to believe, however, that it is a sort of mental poison that has the power to induce confused thinking and that under its sway we are more than apt to eventually resume the use of alcohol.

Anger is antagonistic to our philosophy. It overrides reason. Rehabilitation of an alcoholic "marks time" and progress stops so long as anger dominates. Various degrees of anger ranging from indignation to fury indicate diversified hazards to the member who makes his mind and actions subject to this strong emotion.

The following quotation from our A.A. Book clearly predicts impending danger to those of us who allow ourselves to become bitterly provoked: "If we were to live we had to be free from anger. The grouch and the brainstorm were not for us. They may be the dubious luxury of normal men, but for alcoholics these things are poison."

A simple analysis of this emotion should curb our further indulgences. In it the impulse to injure either friend or enemy is always present. When fully aroused the end use of this impulse is to kill.

The alcoholic is only human. He will be subject to all human impulses and often faced by conditions that arouse him, but he need not be ignorant of the treacherous nature of anger or the insidious inroads its impulses can make upon his recovery.

In compiling our inventories let us keep in mind the fact that we are alcoholics, that we are sick physically, mentally, and spiritually; that we have been unable to recover from our illness through our own efforts, but that thousands of alcoholics before us have effected their recovery by exchanging their alcoholic personalities for the happy, sober personalities brought about by the A.A. way of living. With this in mind, we call upon a *Power Greater than Ourselves* to help guide us in making a searching and fearless moral inventory of ourselves as one of the steps necessary for our recovery.

BLIND SPOTS

At this point it is advisable to face the fact that, notwithstanding our sincere effort to honestly inventory all of "the flaws in our make-up that caused our failure," some will not be recorded. Why? Simply because we fail to see them. Our mental and moral vision has too long been blinded by alcoholic reservation and rationalization.

It is suggested that a blank space be reserved in our inventories for the blind spots we will later uncover. We should not worry about these undisclosed defects. It is well however to be open minded about their existence and let A.A. as a *"Way of Life"* reveal them. We then list them for correction.

SUMMARIZATION — Having decided to let God direct our will and unmanageable lives, we step out of the "Driver's Seat" to inspect our alcoholic personalities. We make "a searching and fearless moral inventory of ourselves," *not as psychiatrists but as sick laymen* who need a simple understanding of our ills and defects—things that God will sublimate or help us outgrow. A.A. personality changes begin from such honest evaluation.

Pages 76 through 83 in the book, "Alcoholics Anonymous," suggest certain character defects, common to alcoholics, which should be listed in a written inventory. From our inventories we learn the spiritual illness of resentment and dishonesty; the frustration of jealously, suspicion, self-pity, fear, anger and false pride; the harmful nature of criticism, intolerance and vindictiveness.

We vitalize our deadened consciences as we catalog our devastating self-centered habits. We develop discernment of right and wrong and stop injuring ourselves and others by elimination of our listed defects. We make our inventory an honest, written one. It may be the difference between sobriety and another drunk.

STEP FIVE—*Admitted to God, to ourselves and to another human being the exact nature of our wrongs.*

If we have been honest and thorough with our personal inventory we have listed and analyzed our character defects and have a record of the harm we have caused others.

We have a list of our greater handicaps and imperfections and also the names of the people who have suffered as a result of our unmanageable lives and insane behavior.

These facts indicate certain defects in our lives; they constitute the record we have made of our wrongs. We have ascertained our weak spots and not only proposed to erase them, but also to prepare a plan of action that will bring restitution and happiness to the men and women who have suffered mental, physical, or financial harm as a direct result of our uncontrolled drinking.

Step Five is a preparatory step to the restitution that we expect to make as we carry out the provisions of Step Nine, where amends are necessary and we make them.

The exact nature of our wrongs now are admitted to God and ourselves and then talked over with a *third person.*

Alcoholic rationalization balks at this honest procedure, discounting the need of admitting anything to *Another Human Being.*

The founders of our movement knew the value of doing this; they knew that only by so doing could we acquire the humility and spiritual inspiration necessary to continuous development in A.A. living.

Most of us felt that our self appraisals were exacting and because we had conceded to God the error of our former alcoholic thought and conduct we saw no need to go farther. We reasoned that God knew; that He would forgive us and so the matter was closed.

This is sugar-coated alcoholic thinking. It follows the old pattern and is but a pretense, a new form of escape from responsibility. We must give our long hoarded secrets to another person if we are to gain peace of mind, confidence, and self respect.

The humility this step brings us is necessary to our future welfare. We will have no spiritual inspiration, no release from anxiety and fear until we remove the skeletons from our closet. We are to stop dodging people and start facing facts and issues if freedom from dread and tension is to be ours.

Step Five is a pivotal step. It calls for action that starts a real spiritual awakening as we back up our FAITH with VERBAL WORKS.

If this step seems difficult to you, (and it may well seem that way) remember that you are no exception. Many of us experienced the same reaction. This reaction is nothing more than the reflexes of a dying alcoholic personality trying to avoid reality—too little time has elapsed between our sudden change from an alcoholic's rationalization to that of rehabilitative conduct necessary to our program. We unconsciously are being dominated by our old thoughts. These are but momentary thoughts of rebellion. They will quickly give way to the sublimating power of our new philosophy if we will be open-minded and have faith that God will aid us in arriving at the right solution.

The step specifically outlines the action to be taken. When the right time arrives, arrange

an interview with anyone outside of A.A.*
who will be *"understanding but unaffected"*
by your narration. We should not take this
step with anyone who might not respect our
confidences. For this reason the clergyman,
psychiatrist or doctor is our best bet. Most
men of these callings are qualified and will
be honored by the confidence placed in them
when they hear our story.

There is no stated time for taking this step
—it is not to be rushed into. We do not take
it as a form that must be complied with. There
is a state of mind that will arise in all sincere
members who "lose themselves" in A.A. philosophy which will indicate clearly when they
are ready. When this time arrives, however,
we must act at once. To postpone taking it is
inconsistent with our plan of recovery.

If in doubt about when to take Step Five—
take it immediately. It is far better to take it
before you think you are ready than to postpone it and then not take it at all. Many members with years of sobriety in A.A. find that
taking Step Five from time to time helps them

* See page 86, paragraphs 2 and 3 in the book, "ALCOHOL-
ICS ANONYMOUS."

to maintain their contented sobriety. Step Five brings mental and spiritual catharsis and should be taken periodically.

You are now engaged in a business deal with God and another human being. If your inventory has been thorough, "you are in a position to pocket your pride," to tell a story "that will illuminate every twist of character, every dark cranny of the past." You have no reason to doubt the psychological and spiritual value offered. You will be well rewarded for your effort and will find yourself at a loss to express in words the gratification that will be yours. *Understanding of such things comes only with experience.*

Interpretation of the deep significance of admitting our wrongs to God, ourselves and another human being is logically summed up by saying, "Once we have taken this step, withholding nothing, we are delighted. We can look the world in the eye. We begin to feel the nearness of our Creator. *We have had* certain spiritual beliefs, but Now WE BEGIN TO HAVE A SPIRITUAL EXPERIENCE."*

*Read page 87 in the book, "ALCOHOLICS ANONYMOUS."

SUMMARIZATION—The metamorphosis from the alcoholic to the NEW A.A. PERSONALITY becomes more evident upon completion of Step Five. We are impressed with the simplicity of this effective spiritual device which has been the means of starting within us a spiritual awakening. The step is a direct challenge to our sincerity, inasmuch as we have been promised humility and a spiritual experience when we have talked over our defects with a third person.

This is the one step in the program that advises you what to do when you have completed it. This advice is given in our A.A. Book. It says, "Returning home we find a place where we can be quiet for an hour, carefully reviewing what we have done. We thank God from the bottom of our hearts that we know Him better. Taking this book down from our shelf we turn to the pages which contain the Twelve Steps. Carefully reading the first five proposals we ask if we have omitted anything, for we are building *An Arch Through Which We Will Walk a Free Man at Last.* Is our work

solid so far? Are the stones properly in place?
Have we skimped on the cement put into the
foundation? Have we tried to make mortar
without sand? If we can answer to our satisfaction, we can then look to Step Six."*

*Read pages 87-88 in the book, "ALCOHOLICS ANONY-
MOUS."

STEP SIX—*We were entirely ready to have God remove all these defects of character.**

STEP SEVEN—*Humbly ask Him to remove our shortcomings.*

———

It is only after we have completed Step Five, when humility has been experienced and self-respect has been restored as a result of our admitting to God and to another human being the exact nature of our wrongs, that we are in a suitable spiritual condition to sincerely carry out the provisions of Steps Six and Seven.

This action brings a heretofore unknown feeling of moral strength. For the first time we are facing our *Real Selves*—the selves whose withered roots have touched and are now drawing up an unfailing source of assurance, power and security.

We find in the consummation of these steps a *New Peace*, a release from *Tension* and *Anxiety* as we now are laying our misconceptions or defeats of character in God's hands. We are asking Him to rid them from our lives. We are exerting great mental cooperation with

* Note paragraphs 2 and 3, page 88, in the book, "ALCOHOLICS ANONYMOUS."

90

God. We feel an intense humility that cries out for recognition and Divine Help.

The *Spiritual Lift*, the nearness to our Creator that is experienced from humble invocation of His help and our willingness to be freed from old willful thoughts and habits are all essential to successful attainment of these steps.

The mental hygiene and spiritual house-cleaning we have started in our inventories and continued in Step Five reaches its climax in Step Seven when we fully subject our wills to God and wish to surrender to Him all of our moral imperfections.

The several objectives of Steps Six and Seven are:

1. To gain an intimate contact with this *Power Greater than Ourselves.*

2. To perfect ourselves in the practice of unselfish prayer.

3. To be aware of our defective character traits.

4. To desire their removal.

5. To surrender completely all defects of character.

6. To believe that God *can* remove them.

7. To ask Him to take them *all away*.

The results we expect from pursuit of these objectives are:

1. A reconciliation to God's way of doing business. We become "fed up" with our way and with further practice of our defective character traits.

2. A willingness to work out a plan for suppression of self-centeredness through gaining a conscious contact with God.

3. To experience dissatisfaction and remorse as a result of our alcoholic practices and to seek a spiritual inspiration that will bring us an inner sense of poise and security.

4. Increased faith, clean hearts and minds, ability to offer unselfish prayer.

5. A spiritual courage that is fearless in its outlook on life; a desire to make restitution to those our drinking has harmed.

6. A desire to quit bluffing and honestly give God a chance to remove from our lives all that stands in the way of our usefulness to Him and to others.

7. Elimination of our defective character traits, acquisition of peace of mind and sobriety.

The spiritual attitude and satisfactory frame of mind necessary to effective fulfillment of these steps has been progressively worked toward in the completion of the first five steps in our program.

Knowledge of our illness alcoholism prompts us to turn to God for help. The alcoholic must pray. There is no standard form of prayer to use. Our remorse over past mistakes and a genuine desire to correct them will indicate how we shall pray.

We all come before God as sick people. We offer no alibis. We have no defense. We stand before Him subject to the weaknesses of alcoholism. We ask for an understanding of this illness and for His strength and help in arresting it. We wish to arrest it, but only for unselfish purposes. We ask forgiveness for the wrongs we have committed. We ask for protection from self-pity, from resentment, from all selfishness. We ask for wisdom and understanding to know His will. We ask for spiritual and physical strength to execute His will. Acknowledging our shortcomings, we sincerely pray to God that He will remove them.

Prayer is a three-way contact with God. By it we ask, receive and acknowledge. We thank Him now for our sobriety, for A.A. and its founders.

There is nothing outstanding about an alcoholic's prayer to God. It is just a simple sincere affair in which the alcoholic has nothing to lose but from which he gains SOBRIETY — SANE BEHAVIOR — PEACE OF MIND — AND HAPPINESS FOR HIMSELF AND FAMILY.

There is a latent power within each of us that develops through conscious contact with God. It replaces alcoholic fear and weakness with spiritual strength and understanding. Through It, the miracle of A.A. is possible.

Steps Six and Seven utilize this contact which thousands of alcoholics have humbly used in removing their defects of character.

In these two steps are found the forge in which we heat and form the separate links that go into the new personality chains we are building. *Without them our rehabilitation is impossible.*

SUMMARIZATION—Restoration of our mental and spiritual health is in direct proportion to our recognized need for help and our willingness to work for recovery. Brain damage and reservations are the only limitations to our recovery.

Reservations are identified as those mental attitudes opposed to self-evaluation, co-operation, honesty, tolerance, forgiveness, faith, love and unselfish prayer. These "character defects" stand between us and contented sobriety. They perpetuate spiritual illness. Recovery from alcoholism is dependent upon their removal.

A divine type of surgery is suggested by Steps Numbers Six and Seven. Humble prayer becomes the spiritual scalpel with which God cuts out the damaged portions of our sick personalities. Complete surrender assures us a painless, successful operation.

Surrender of our "Defects" to a "Higher Power" is not the spiritless act of a defeatist, but the intelligent act of an alcoholic who would replace his fear and weakness with spiritual courage, understanding, strength and contented sobriety. "Humbly ask Him to remove our shortcomings."

STEP EIGHT—*Made a list of all the people we had harmed and become willing to make amends to them all.**

STEP NINE—*Made direct amends to such people wherever possible, except when to do so would injure them or others.*

————

The objective of Steps Eight and Nine is to *outline* and put into *practice* a working course of conduct which will directly rectify the harm or injury our drinking may have imposed upon others, at the same time start harmoniously relating us to life and to our fellow men.

The practice of the Alcoholics Anonymous philosophy adequately fulfills these requirements. It is a proved *"Way of Life"* by which the alcoholic corrects his past mistakes and makes restitution to relative, friend, or enemy as he effects his own recovery from the physical, mental and spiritual ravages of alcoholism.

Many alcoholics agree to the effectiveness of our philosophy but fail to benefit from it because they have not properly evaluated their

* Study pages 88 to 96 inclusive in the book, "ALCOHOLICS ANONYMOUS."

alcoholic illness. Not believing themselves to be sick, they see no reason for inconveniencing themselves to get well. Reservations as to their spiritual illness create indifference to the "Making of Amends."

Members do not arrest alcoholism or gain recovery by merely agreeing with the principles of A.A. philosophy — *They Recover Only if They Live Them.*

These steps work in conjunction with each other. We have a list of those we have harmed —we have our grudge list—we have a list of those we are financially obligated to. Few of us realize that our own names head the list of those we have wronged and that by living this program we are first making amends to ourselves, to our outraged constitutions, to our confused minds, and to our troubled spirits.

It is not a difficult thing to list the people who suffered because we drank. Our real problem is to arrive at a state of mind that concedes the damage we have done and embraces a sincere willingness to amend it.

Step Nine is not easily or quickly carried out. Some restitution is started upon our acceptance of the A.A. program as a *"Way of*

Life." This is usually quite limited as it is not until we have spent several months in A.A. and have fortified our sobriety with good fundamental knowledge of the program that we acquire the spiritual courage and understanding to dispense reparations discreetly.

The member is confronted with many obstacles in observance of this step. We find procrastination a hindrance to some members. This should be avoided. On the other hand, there are those who are too ambitious to rebuild, to get the thing over with at once. Remember, that in most cases you will require a lifetime to complete Step Nine. Some members under inspiration of the new personalities they are creating become emotional and act on the spur of the moment. Their hasty action is apt to fall short of accomplishment. Pride is another barrier. Confusion, through improper interpretation of the purpose of this step, is a common handicap.

The older members will be helpful, if consulted, wherever perplexities are encountered. Do not act hastily or in doubt — invite their opinions—then formulate a plan of action with God and start making right the wrongs for which you are responsible.

Meditation and prayer are necessary in order to make amends. No amend should be made that is not preceded by prayer as it will lack complete purpose and effectiveness. Conscious contact with God in the matter of making amends will not only bring about a more satisfactory result, but will also aid you in determining those amends to avoid which might injure others. Discretion in this connection is imperative.*

God's presence in our lives now alters and sublimates our mental and physical activities. It gives us the humility we need to make amends and an incentive to get started. *"We Are Trying to Put Our Lives in Order. We Do This Through Maximum Service to God and the People About Us."*

The question now arises: Whose names belong on our list? How do we go about it in making amends to these people? What procedure do we follow?

Our answers to these questions are found in the Alcoholics Anonymous Book on pages 88 to 96 inclusive.

The following summary of certain advice taken from those pages is incomplete and must

*Read par. 3, page 91 — par. 2, page 92 in the book, "ALCOHOLICS ANONYMOUS."

be enlarged upon by each member in application to his particular needs.

We find it impossible to cover this complex matter in its entirety, but have listed a few suggestions and examples for guidance. Our list classifies four types of people and comments on a fifth who is not generally included in the list to whom amends are made, yet who must constantly be considered, if permanent sobriety is to be assured.

GROUP ONE—FRIENDS

In this group are the people who have been close friends, business associates, etc., those toward whom we should be friendly, but have severed connections with because of resentments, pride, or fancied wrongs, the ones we have treated unjustly but have not harmed aside from harsh words or acts of asinine behavior, and with whom indebtedness is not a consideration.

The technique to be observed in approaching the people in this class is based on sincerity. Our approach is "calm, frank and open." We aim to convince the party of our good intentions and to assure him that we regret the treatment he has received at our hands.

We explain our alcoholic illness, the nature of resentments and hatred in relation to our sobriety. We outline our good intentions and ask forgiveness and cooperation in our future associations. Our purpose is to create good will and regain friendship.

We avoid impressing anyone with the idea that we are religious fanatics, but we never sidestep the spiritual issue or deny God if He is brought into the conversation.

We do not attempt amends to those "who are still smarting from a recent injustice" and never make any amends that will harm another person.

There will be few cases where our advances are rejected. If we are unable to establish a reconciliation and are not favorably received, we simply drop the matter in hopes that eventually our sobriety and future dealings will repair the breach between us.

The main point to keep in mind is that we are out to perform a duty, that we will not be upset or discouraged by gruff or unpleasant receptions, that the intent of our visit is a harmonious one and that *Under No Consideration Will We Live in an Angry or Resentful Mood.*

GROUP TWO—FAMILIES*

The people under this group are generally found in our families. The outstanding examples are the wives of the alcoholics, or in the case of the alcoholic women, the husbands. Then follow the mothers, fathers, sons, daughters, and often close friends whose lives we have "kept in turmoil because of our selfish and inconsiderate habits." We have been "like a tornado roaring our way through the lives of others," breaking hearts and "killing sweet relationships." The damage we have done to this group has been spread over many years. It will take many years to undo it.

Our approach technique is no problem here unless homes have been broken up and separation makes reparation contacts impossible. Even then the member will benefit from living the program as his record of sobriety usually comes to the attention of the injured one. Time may be required to effect reconciliation, but

* Read pages 135 to 149 inclusive in the book, "ALCO-HOLICS ANONYMOUS."

satisfactory adjustments are generally forth-coming. Often this has been handled through correspondence, but direct contact is prefera-ble in all cases wherever possible.

If the home is still intact the member's fam-ily is aware of his desire to treat his alcoholic illness and seldom fails to back him up in this purpose.

It is important that they read the book, "Alcoholics Anonymous," to gain an under-standing of alcoholism and the steps outlined in our program for its treatment. A new mem-ber needs the full understanding and cooper-ation of his family. His amends to them are most thorough and are made with greater ease when they realize what he is trying to do.

Our sobriety is a blessing to the individuals in Group Two. As a rule, it is the greatest single amend we can make them, yet it is a partial amend that must be followed up with kind and thoughtful acts.* Sobriety in itself is not enough. We must be attentive and con-siderate of the family as a whole. Harmony and cooperation must be established. Evidence of our love and a desire to become worthy of

* A review of the chapter to wives, page 117, in the book, "ALCOHOLICS ANONYMOUS," will prove helpful.

their respect will be most helpful. Irreparable damage is not unusual. When encountered it can only be offset by obvious manifestation of our willingness to right the condition if it were possible. We lose no time in making the amends that are possible.

Sex problems complicate the lives of many alcoholics. The first consideration in handling them is to stop the trouble at its source. Honesty is a prime factor in the lives of all members and leaves no room for adultery.

Injury to others must be considered in straightening out our sex problems. We always use great tact in handling the situation if amends are in order. Jealousy, when aroused, greatly impedes our progress. Fairness, meditation, and prayer must be relied upon. We lay the matter in God's hands and are then guided by the dictates of His inspiration and will.

GROUP THREE—CREDITORS

"We do not dodge our creditors."* The creditor usually knows about our drinking. If not, we should "lay our cards on the table."

* Read paragraph 4, page 90, in the book, "ALCOHOLICS ANONYMOUS."

If payment is impossible, arrange the best deal
we can. It may be a future date when we will
start paying or possibly we can pay even small
amounts until we become financially able to
increase them. The main idea is *to have an
understanding*. We must be at ease in this connection, otherwise fear may return us to drinking. When the creditor understands the nature
of our alcoholic illness he will readily see that
money cannot be forthcoming unless we maintain sobriety and thus be in a better mood to
receive our proposition.

GROUP FOUR—THE DECEASED

The harm we have done to departed relatives or friends is often a cause for self-con-
demnation. This should not be; it is a harmful
practice that is unwise because there is no
remedy for it.

We must realize the futility of remorse
over wrongs that we cannot amend. We do not
allow such errors of the past to impair our future usefulness. We reason that the harm done
will be partly offset by the new philosophy
we are living. That inasmuch as we cannot
reach the departed one we can still make

amends to living relatives. If this is impossible we resort to God in prayer, asking Him to see the willingness in our hearts and to forgive us in connection with these people.

Then there are *the amends we must daily make to God*. These become automatic; they are the requirements of each of the Twelve Steps. The A.A. program is *One Big Amend* broken up into twelve parts.

Before we can settle for the harm done others we must eliminate the source of moral and physical devastation to ourselves.

Alcoholism is our illness. It accounts for the imposition of injury upon our families, friends, and those loved ones who have departed. It accounts for our indebtedness; it is responsible for our impaired physical condition; it has brought us irrational thinking, insane behavior, and spiritual illness.

We make amends to ourselves, to the personalities we were before becoming alcoholic, by understanding our sickness, by illuminating our defects of character, by eliminating them from our lives, by intelligent physical care of our bodies, by restoration of our men-

tal apparatus through sobriety, and by treatment of our spiritual illness through recourse
to understanding and practice of God's Will.
The alcoholic's rehabilitation is contingent upon amends and will be *As Long As He Lives.*

We often are inclined to clutter up our list
with petty wrongs long forgotten and of no
great importance. Amends of this sort would
never end; they should be forgotten. Many of
us have been uncertain over the advisability
of making some amends. The yardstick to use
in this connection is your conscience; if the
wrong bothers you it should undoubtedly be
amended.

The people covered in this discussion will
not comprise a full list of those to whom we
make amends. There will be others on our list
and we will find that new errors constantly oc-
curing in our lives will send us back to make
reparation to those already on the list.

Step Nine has reclaimed many broken
friendships; it has brought peace and happiness to the lives of those who suffered because
of our alcoholism. Its great rehabilitative
power has also affected the lives of thousands
of alcoholics through the spiritual awakening

they have experienced. Because of this step, these same alcoholics have recovered their self-respect, they have taken on courage and confidence, and they have assumed responsibility. They sense God's presence and with His presence comes the realization that their lives are again becoming manageable.

SUMMARIZATION — The importance of "Amends" to an alcoholic's sobriety is easily underestimated. Manifold benefits are ours when we assume this creative personal responsibility. It quickens moral vitality, mental health, spiritual development. It integrates the personality through harmonious relations with God, with the people about us and with the circumstances of everyday living.

Sobriety alone cannot do this. It is only a partial amend. It pays no bills and offers little restitution to those we have harmed. Unwillingness to make amends often furthers their injury by filling us with discontent, belligerency and may result in continued drunkenness.

Contented sobriety is our only hope for recovery. We earn it with honesty and "Right motives." We come clean with God and the people listed in our inventory. We pay our creditors. Enliven our conscience with prayer and meditation. Start making "Amends" we owe, avoiding those that might harm others. Are willing and thorough, remembering that temporary sobriety is the consequence of half-way compliance with Steps Numbers Eight and Nine.

STEP TEN—*Continued to take personal inventory and when we were wrong promptly admitted it.**

Step Ten is one of the maintenance steps. Its purpose is to remind us that the moral defects we have recognized in selfishness, dishonesty, resentment, and fear are still problems we daily encounter; that they remain serious threats to our sobriety. A.A. suggests a daily inventory to disclose our harmful thoughts and actions. Admitting mistakes is invaluable to this inventory.

George A. Dorsey contributes a bit of interesting information relative to the instability of man's nature by saying, "Man is something happening all the time; he is a going concern, he makes his rules, revises his formulae and recasts his mould in the act of being and while going. *It Is in Man's Nature That He Does Not Stay Put.*"

This step provides a daily self-inventory to check our mental status.

Through it we avoid the unhappy experiences that follow when we are dominated by

* Read pages 96 to 98 inclusive in the book, "ALCOHOLICS ANONYMOUS."

forms of self-centeredness which try to creep back into our lives.

We make the inventory a sort of intelligence department that identifies moral defects both old and new. It is a Rogue's Gallery where we catalogue each defect and its alias so when self-centeredness, for instance, disguises itself in the form of complacency or boredom, we detect the deception and arrest it.

These defects are great sources of danger to us. They had much to do with the injuries once suffered from abnormal drinking. They can still return us to the Insanity of Alcoholism.

Step Four provided us with an inventory that served a definite purpose. It exposed character defects we formerly refused to recognize —defects that made our lives unmanageable. The necessity for listing and removing these personality flaws becomes increasingly obvious as we add new days to our record of sober living.

The inventory supplied us with an understanding of our problem. It brought us face to face with ourselves with our shortcomings— with the sense of removing them through

God's help. It was indispensable at the time but fulfilled its intended use once the nature of our self-willed alcoholic habit and defects were recorded. Without this record, progress in A.A. would have been impossible.

Because of this record, progress has been made. Knowledge of our moral defects and practice of the A.A. program have completely changed our lives, our attitude toward our own problems and our feeling toward our fellow men.

We have gained the confidence and the respect of others. Many of our friends have expressed their admiration of the sobriety we have acquired. Pride and satisfaction naturally follow this accomplishment. We enjoy our security and the friendly attitude of those about us.

Step Ten will safeguard this progress if we continue our personal inventories and promptly admit it when we are wrong.

Let us not forget, however, that alcoholics never seem to stay put. Our founders knew this from their own experiences. They knew that drinking habits of long standing would cry aloud for customary performance privileges.

They knew that new character defects would appear and that many of the old ones would present themselves in disguised form. Hence a daily mental checkup to announce the advent of each old habit and a sort of mental sentry on guard to detect the new ones.

Avoid confusing the respective functions of Steps Four and Ten.

Step Four was a written inventory listing our alcoholic character defects and the people we had harmed. We left it open for future additions.

Step Ten is the A.A. slide rule for quick mental reckoning of daily A.A. progress—a perpetual mental inventory that safeguards our waking hours of sobriety—with which we close each day.

The plan of our philosophy is to *live each step*. The object of Step Ten is not only to continue our personal inventory, but also to check daily the progress we are making with each step in the A.A. program.

By reviewing them we often find ourselves "off the beam." This is a bad spot for an alcoholic who invariably goes whole hog if immediate steps toward correction are not taken.

Correction is possible if we realize our danger when our inventories reveal it to us. Prompt action upon such discovery is necessary. It is not unusual to find ourselves off the beam—the idea is to get back on again. The inventory is essential to this requirement.

In order that all members may recognize a few of the "off the beam" positions it may be well to list them:

1. When we have forgotten that we are alcoholics — that we have a nervous system which is incapable of withstanding the "soothing influence" of alcohol.

2. When complacency lowers our guard and allows resentment and intolerance to creep back into our lives.

3. When we ease up on the practice of honesty, humility and making amends.

4. When we become cocky over our A.A. success and cease contact with God.

5. When we lack interest in new members and feel it inconvenient to help them.

6. When we become irked with meetings and peevish with other members.

7. When boredom makes an appearance.

8. When we start missing A.A. meetings.

9. When we travel without the A.A. Book.

When the inventory discloses that we show any of these symptoms we may be sure that one of our outstanding troubles is self-centeredness. Further investigation will unearth a severe case of spiritual congestion.

The antidote for these troubles is to apply ourselves to a close study of our program. Read the book. Talk A.A. with the members. Sincerely interest ourselves in our A.A. group. Attend more meetings. Do our bit. Consider our alcoholism as arrested but never cured. Lose ourselves in the program. Work with new members. Review the miracle that God has performed in our lives. Be honest and thankfully offer a prayer of appreciation. Always carry the A.A. Book on out of town trips.

The second part of Step Ten, *"When We Were Wrong, Promptly Admitted It,"* is not to be taken lightly. It is a good character conditioner. Recognition of a wrong is not enough; verbal acknowledgement should follow. The requirements of our program are to make amends if the wrong has harmed anyone. The inventory keeps us alert to our responsibility in this matter.

The sincere member will apply these things to himself. He will search out the significance of "Admitting It When He Is Wrong."

Do you remember in Step Five when we admitted to God, to ourselves, and to another human being the exact nature of our wrongs? How we meditated our shortcomings in Steps Six and Seven? How vital it was to our well-being at the time?

It is still vital. We haven't changed in that respect and we never will. Alcoholism has been arrested, but we have not been cured.

It is not in the nature of the alcoholic to stay put. We must admit our wrongs to receive the feeling of decency and worthiness that keeps us in the right mental and spiritual condition to maintain contented permanent sobriety.

Continue this inventory daily. When we are wrong let us understand the value of getting it off our chests at once. Admit our mistakes. It is stupid to defend our blunders. Get rid of that habit.* Remember that our *New Personality Is Not Compatible with Moral Defects or Concealed Errors.*

It makes us more self-critical and less apt to criticize others. It keeps us on the beam.

We do not make a farce of our lives when we employ our inventories. We should check ourselves thoroughly to make real headway. We owe it to God, to ourselves and our families. We must think sober to live sober.

The inventory will help us to know just what degree of success we are attaining in A.A. It will let us know where we stand. It will keep us in *Good Standing.*

---

* Observance and practice of this step will give you knowledge and develop your capacity to use it. Step 10 will create a stable mental balance most helpful to a better spiritual condition so necessary in your recovery from alcoholism.

SUMMARIZATION—Nothing is more important to the recovering alcoholic than the maintenance of contented sobriety.

Step Ten affords such maintenance. It is a simple, effective means of sounding the hazardous shoals of mental drunkenness for reservations, thoughts, moods or acts by which we might be returned to physical drunkenness. Self-centeredness remains a dire threat.

We safeguard our daily sobriety by frequent mental audits as to our behavior and willingness to admit mistakes. We make the personal inventory a daily habit. It will uncover much negative thought and willful behavior for correction by the dictates of our conscience. By closing the day with a review of our emotional conduct and our treatment of others, we can discover and correct both our willfulness and mistakes.

Admitting our mistakes brings both psychological and spiritual benefits. They complement the personal inventory. They quicken our conscience, alerting us to knowledge of our need for God's help; for divine sublimation of our wills; for continued practice of Step Ten.

STEP ELEVEN—*Sought through prayer and meditation to improve our conscious contact with God as we understood Him, praying only for knowledge of His will for us and the power to carry that out.*

This step can be broken down into three parts. Let us first consider that part which recommends the need for prayer and meditation to improve our understanding of God, our contact with Him.

A prayer for improved contact with God, for knowledge of His will, and for mental, physical and spiritual energy to carry it out, requires the coordinated effort of all our faculties.

Knowledge of the need of this step is based on the past experience of A.A. members, *some of whom have demonstrated the ability to forget that they Have Not Been Cured of Alcoholism.* They have mistaken recovery for cure, so after a few months of sobriety have considered practice of the A.A. philosophy unnecessary. They have overlooked the fact that the human mind was not constituted to remember the pain and sorrow suffered from disease. They take their changed personalities *Too*

Much for Granted, assuming that once acquired they will always stay with them.

God's help was needed in their dire emergency, but that is passed now. They say, "We will never drink again, we never even think about it." They let down their guard and ease up on spiritual contacts and service.

A positive attitude toward permanent sobriety is commendable, but only recommended as it applies to each twenty-four hour period.

The fact we have no desire or intention to ever drink again is a favorable frame of mind for the new member to hold. It is our ambition, a mental condition to be grateful for, *But One That Too Often Fosters Complacency Which Can Lead Us into Trouble Unless God Is Given Full Credit for the Sobriety We Enjoy.*

When complacency develops we are apt to forget the part that God has played in effecting our rehabilitation. We overlook the fact that our nervous systems are still those of alcoholics. We seem to forget that as alcoholics we are susceptible to moods and emotions that we formerly appeased with alcohol. Complacency obscures the knowledge that our recovery from alcoholism was granted by a *Power Greater than Ourselves*, that without contact with God, reversion to our old low physical and spiritual levels is probable.

Cooperation with a *Power Greater than Ourselves* has pulled us out of the alcoholic rut. Step Eleven is a maintenance step that was planned to keep us out and to make us stay put.

It keeps us spiritually active and in tune with God. It insures against the dulling of inspiration as our alcoholic problems diminish.

Understanding of this situation and the knowledge that members do get "off the beam" spiritually at times is our first line of defense We fortify this defense by keeping uppermost in our minds that "In reality we are on a *Daily Reprieve*, that our reprieves are *Contingent Upon Our Spiritual Condition.*"*

The bitter experiences of members who insist upon learning the hard way—the backsliders who returned to drinking—attest to the truth of this statement.

*Read page 97 in the book, "ALCOHOLICS ANONYMOUS."

Invariably their trouble *First Starts with Neglect of Prayer* and matures when they completely abandon conscious contact with God and service to others.

Our realization of God's help in the past impresses us with the fact that it can be utilized to even better use in the future. A sure way of increasing this help and expanding our contact with God is possible through simple prayers of sincere appreciation. Meditate on the help He has given, acknowledge its source, and be genuine in your thanks for His understanding of your alcoholic problem and the strength He has given you to overcome it.

He has demonstrated a miracle in our lives, so our problem no longer is entirely one of achievement. We have acquired sobriety and are enjoying its benefits. Through it we have regained health and mental normalcy and have built up self-respect within ourselves, at home, and among our friends. It is our privilege and duty to safeguard and protect this miracle. It was accomplished through humility, faith, and prayer as we actively tried to understand and carry out His will.

Prayers of appreciation are not all that we

indulge in, but they are unselfish and are the quickest means of bringing us into His presence. Contacting God with thanks and appreciation will supply fast inspiration that goes a long way toward improving our understanding and nearness to Him. Such contacts renew our faith and keep us active.

Each member will naturally have his own technique for improving his contact with God, but if actual prayers of appreciation are missing, the technique should be enlarged to include them. It is more sensible to ask for a required circumstance after you have acknowledged and expressed thanks for receiving a previous one.

Prayer and meditation to improve our conscious contact with God seem easiest when we are relaxed and composed (when strife, fear and resentment are laid aside) and we are in harmony with those about us. For this reason it is advisable to consider the importance of mental composure and physical relaxation insofar as prayer is concerned, and to further comment upon them as stabilizers to the restless nature of the alcoholic.

The point in mind is that the Twelve Steps

will lead many of us to recognize our need for spiritual help, but will not direct attention to the fact we may be abusing our source of physical and mental energy.

Relaxation of mind and body and surrender of our will to God are undoubtedly necessary before satisfactory prayer and meditation are engaged in.

We owe God both humility and respect; we show it by freeing ourselves, for the moment, from material consideration, from self-pity, fear or anxiety, and by giving Him our undivided attention.

It is profitable for us to understand the value of keeping our bodies in a healthy condition, to practice poise and composure.

The alcoholic is apt to possess a restless disposition that tends toward over-activity.   He not only practiced this by uncontrolled drinking, but showed evidence of his intemperance in many other ways. Therefore we recommend relaxation as an aid to prayer and suggest that a quiet time, aside from prayer, will be beneficial to all alcoholics.*

*Read page 100 in the book,"ALCOHOLICS ANONYMOUS."

The habit of relaxation practiced during quiet times at intervals throughout each day is exactly what we need. Prominent medical authorities agree on this matter.

The intervals will be determined by our moods and mental attitudes, by our response to fear, anger, fatigue, emotional stress, or whenever we feel the pressure of high nerve tension.

The ill effects of these things upon the alcoholic's mental condition decidedly regulate his behavior. They constitute a hazard that jeopardizes his chances of recovery.

These are the things he once relieved by drinking. He cannot ignore them now, and expect to function normally or attain that degree of spiritual or mental efficiency which composure would bring.

How do we do this? We attempt to suspend momentarily all mental and physical activities. We try to relax our entire bodies, then close our minds to the worries and anxieties about us.

What do we think about? Nothing. Let go of everything, just rest and learn to *"Take It Easy."*

How long do we continue this? Be your own judge. It can be a matter of minutes if necessary. We know, however, from experience, that even *Thirty Seconds of Complete Relaxation* of mind and body will do the trick. It is simple. Try it.

You owe it to yourself and to the people about you. Your conscious contact with God is hardly complete without it.

The second part of this step deals with *Prayer for a Knowledge of His Will.* This knowledge will bring the proper use of our will, which seems to be tied up in self-denial and willing service to others.

The question that has repeatedly confronted members is—*What Is God's Will?—How Am I to Know It from My Own Will?*

God's will for the alcoholic primarily concerns the treatment of an incurable illness: Alcoholism. It embraces relationship with God, sobriety, understanding, honesty, humility, love and service.

Members should quickly realize that the A.A. philosophy is not a religion. A.A. is a practical therapy for arresting the disease alcoholism. The practice of the Twelve Steps in no way conflicts with any religion. Daily practice of all Twelve Steps, however, is essential to the understanding of God's will by the alcoholic.

The will of God would be more easily understood and executed if there was no one in the world but yourself to consider.

You would not lie to yourself as you do under the present circumstances; cheating would not only be unnecessary, it would be impossible. You could not commit adultery and there would be no excuse or occasion for leading a double life.

Drunkenness under such circumstances would not harm anyone but yourself. Moral values would be entirely changed, making sin impossible unless you denied God completely. The nature of our prayers would have little resemblance to the prayers we now offer. The chief need we would have for God then would be that of personal contact to offset loneliness, to avert danger, to cure sickness, and to establish security in the world hereafter.

Such self-centered living would soon become boresome beyond belief. We would long for human companionship. Someone to share our lives, to hear our tales of woe, and to minister to. Our successes and reverses would mean little unless we could share them. **Man's happiness stems from faith in God, from creative endeavor, from a desire to live and let live. That is the way God made him and he cannot fulfill his destiny otherwise.** Fortunately we are not alone in this universe but are one of millions that are entirely dependent upon each other for the necessities of life and the peace of mind that makes living worth while.

We, therefore, deduct that our understanding of God's will *starts with surrender of our wills to Him and with charitable, loving acts of service to others.* "We cannot live unto ourselves alone."

The worthwhile spiritual experience all of us have had really came after we had renounced self-will and were admitting our wrongs, making amends, or performing charitable deeds that benefited others at the expense of our time and money. It was only while engaged in thought and activity of this nature that we keenly felt the presence of God, or came close to the knowledge of His will. The answer to our prayer for such understanding comes with the least effort when we are busy on spiritual missions of help and service to our families and friends, or when we are at work with new members. Our efforts in this direction, aided by faith and prayer for guidance have brought us near to God.

Daily practice of the Alcoholics Anonymous program keeps us close to the spiritual and physical needs of humanity. There is much work to be done in its rehabilitation, as we interest ourselves in this work and carry it on, *We Are, to the Best of Our Ability and Knowledge, Gaining an Understanding of God's Will Through the Service We Render Others.*

The active member who is trying to carry the will of God into his daily life should never become discouraged when he is criticized at home or by fellow members of the organization, *so long as his motives are sincere and constructive.* If he is wrong, he admits it and seeks further understanding from God. He keeps on trying. Faith in his work and prayer must be maintained.

Appreciation of this situation is necessary by all members. None of us should question the works of another *unless we know the motive behind them is foreign to God's will.*

Criticism, even when in order, should be of

a constructive nature. When offered it should be of cooperative intent, not the result of resentment or envy.

The older members make moves or advocate policies that are generally sound and wise as they base them on understanding of past experiences. The newer man may question them and through lack of understanding take a fixed stand against their adoption.

We are, therefore, cautioned against questioning the acts of any member until we know his motive, until we know he is wrong. If he is right we could easily be questioning the will of God. Our purpose is to conform to it, *Never to Oppose It*.

The third part of this step relates to prayer for the power to *Carry Out God's Will*. This prayer is for *Mental Efficiency*, for *Spiritual Strength*, and for *Physical Endurance*.

We must merit the power we seek by first improving our efficiency. Mental energy, spiritual strength, and physical endurance are not granted until we qualify for them. We may pray for them, and we should, but they cannot be had for the asking alone. They must be earned by honest endeavor.

This power is developed as we surrender self-centeredness and by prayer and meditation "We improve our conscious contact with God." When we forgive and help others.

We cannot live their lives but we can help them to help themselves. Our interest will urge them on to renewed effort. As we aid their progress we enrich our own resourcefulness. As we help them develop strength we are unconsciously devising ways and means for gaining new power and understanding ourselves.

It is not wise to pray for power selfishly or with resentment, envy, or self-pity in our hearts. God grants spiritual help freely to honest alcoholics who try to live the A.A. program. His help is limited only by reservations and half-hearted application. Members who faithfully live the Twelve Steps to the best of their ability should pray frequently. God will answer their unselfish prayer.

At times our thinking becomes self-centered. We try to force issues. We mistake our own willfulness for Divine Will and by sheer will power accomplish certain objectives. The true source of such power soon becomes evident. We find ourselves out of harmony with other members. We fail to sense that warm feeling of satisfaction. We lack proper inspiration. We are unappreciated and misunderstood. We are doing things from which we derive no pleasure and which are not particularly useful to others. When this occurs we may be sure that the power we are generating has no connection with the *Power Greater than Ourselves.*

It is safe to use this comparison as a yardstick to gauge the source and quality of our power.

When we get no inspiration or happiness from our efforts we certainly are not in harmony with God or those about us. We should apply Step Ten at once. Admitting our mistakes and praying for spiritual aid will be most helpful. Follow up with outright service to someone else. God releases power to those whose lives are a channel for His will. This takes us out of the "Driver's Seat" and back to the A.A. program

We all suffer from spiritual apathy and misuse of our emotional energy. Perhaps we should restore spiritual balance by retaking Step Five.

Paradoxically the alcoholic's emotions either make or break him. It seems necessary that we learn their constructive use.

There is a practical solution to our emotional problems, a procedure that responds to the intelligent application of facts that science has provided.

Experience teaches us the part our emotional behavior has played in acquiring and maintaining our alcoholic condition. It is generally agreed that feelings of hate, criticism, resentment, self-pity, jealousy and intolerance, and other such manifestations of emotions or feelings prolonged and greatly aggravated the insane behavior of our compulsive drinking.

Psychology teaches us that *Emotions and Feelings Are Sources of Energy*. Examples of this energy are to be found in the emotions of SEX, FEAR, ANGER and LOVE. We are further taught that man must have this emotional energy to function mentally and physically. Without it he would be abnormal.

We are also informed that without the drive of emotional energy man would be a helpless bedridden creature. He would lack the capacity to engage in the daily routine of living. He would not think or move about. He would be practically immobile. He would retain his reflex action, nothing else.

The simple deductions from these facts are that the alcoholic has overlooked the value of harnessing the right emotional energy. He has used the energy of negative power at the expense of positive power.

Obviously, the drive from sex, fear and anger has been instinctively employed. Ironically we have subjugated our wills to them to the detriment of our spiritual well-being. We have not taken the time to visualize our inability to withstand the demands of such devastating energy.

We have overlooked a greater source of energy that we are capable of generating: Love.

Human energy is at its maximum and is most constructive in form when the mind and body are activated by this worthy emotion.

It is reasonable to believe, therefore, that the *Power to Carry Out God's Will Must Come from the Inspiration and Energy That Are to Be Found in the Emotion—Love. Love That Embraces God and Our Fellowmen. Service to and Appreciation of Both.*

SUMMARIZATION—We set up a definite 24-hour discipline of our emotional conduct. We start each day with a morning quiet time praying for freedom from self-centeredness, fear and dishonesty. Planning our day we ask for a knowledge of God's will; for Divine direction that we may make right decisions. Our prayers should be unselfish and useful to others.

This step recommends that we relax and cease foolish waste of energy. Establish a daily period for reading the book, "Alcoholics Anonymous;" read spiritual literature; clear our minds of wrong motives; learn to live and let live.

Each night we inventory our activities of that day. We admit the wrong we have done. We ask God's forgiveness and consult Him regarding amends to be made, closing our day with a prayer of appreciation for His help; for our sobriety.*

* This summarization from pages 98-99-100 in the book, "ALCOHOLICS ANONYMOUS." Study them, then set up your 24 hour schedule of A.A. living.

STEP TWELVE—*Having had a spiritual experience as the result of these steps, we tried to carry this message to alcoholics, and to practice these principles in all our affairs.**

Step Twelve is informative to a high degree, specifically pointing out that a spiritual awakening is possible *only* if we have been living each of the preceding steps, and then suggesting that we draw from our experience and knowledge an objective message which we convey to other interested alcoholics. It further advises us to continue the Alcoholics Anonymous program as a "Design for Living," as our future *"Way of Life."*

Interpretation and practical application of Step Twelve is simply arrived at by separate consideration of the three divisions into which it falls.

FIRST DIVISION

"Having had a spiritual experience as the result of these steps."

The new member is slow to recognize a spiritual experience in his new *"Way of Life;"* in fact, the terms "Spiritual Experience" or "Awakening" often confuse him by diverting

* Read pages 101 to 116 inclusive in the book, "ALCOHOLICS ANONYMOUS."

138

his thoughts from intended A.A. usage to ha-
los, sprouting wings, religion, mystic phe-
nomena, or drastic emotional upheavals.

Reference to pages 399 and 400, in Appendix 2 of the book, "Alcoholics Anonymous,"
clarifies the meanings of these spiritual terms,
explaining t h a t revolutionary character
changes are not common, but that as we do
enlarge upon our spiritual concepts we can
develop a God-consciousness that will entirely
change our reaction toward life and our attitude toward our fellow men.

In arriving at a true picture of this A.A.
metamorphosis it is helpful to reflect upon our
spiritual experience as stepping stones to the
New Personalities we gain by daily practice
of the Twelve Steps.

Most of our experiences are what the psy-
chologist William James calls the "education-
al variety" because *they develop slowly over
a period of time.* Quite often friends of the
newcomer are aware of the difference long before he is himself. He finally realizes that he
has undergone a profound alteration in his reaction to life; that such a change could hardly
have been brought about by himself alone.

We then sense the handiwork of this *Power*

Greater than Ourselves as in a few months we have acquired sobriety, peace of mind and sane behavior that years of self-discipline could not bring.

It takes no great stretch of imagination to allocate the source of power we draw upon in arresting alcoholism; we should have little trouble recognizing, in the awareness of this power, "the essence of spiritual experience."

Evidence of the help God has provided us can be detected in the humility we have acquired, the responsibility we daily assume, the contented sobriety we enjoy, and the unselfish interest we take in aiding fellow alcoholics.

The restraint we exercise with regard to resentment, anger, criticism; the amends we make; our sincerity, honesty, tolerance—these are all possible because of our willingness to accept the spiritual concepts of our program.

Sobriety in itself is a miracle in our case. Looking back over our lives for the past few months we concede a decided improvement in our moral viewpoint. We have developed God-conscious personalities sufficient to effect our recovery from alcoholism. The changes that have made our recovery possible can be identified as spiritual experiences. They have altered seemingly impossible circumstances in our lives.

The outcome of our improved spiritual status and the service we render others is not without benefit. God finally declares a dividend, not in human coinage but in the Divine Currency of Serenity. We are allowed to draw upon an infinite store of harmony and well being. *We become at peace with the world.*

Excerpts from "Our Southern Friend," in the A.A. Book mention this serenity. They say, "God produces harmony in those who receive His Spirit and follow Its dictates. . . . Today when I become more harmonized within, I become more in tune with all of God's wonderful creation. . . . There are periods of darkness, but the stars are shining, no matter how black the night. . . . There are disturbances, but I have learned that if I seek patience and openmindedness, understanding will come. And with it, direction by the Spirit of GOD. The dawn comes and with it more understanding, the peace that passes understanding, and the joy of living that is not disturbed by circumstances or people around me."*

* Read pages 226 to 241 inclusive in the book, "ALCOHOLICS ANONYMOUS."

The cumulative benefits of A.A. living enlarge as we share them with each other. God
has become a daily experience in our lives.
He has given us courage, understanding, appreciation, power and contented sobriety. To
hoard these benefits is to lose them. We maintain our recovery by aiding alcoholics less
fortunate than ourselves.

SECOND DIVISION

*"We tried to carry this message to alco-
holics."*

Purely for reasons of identification and to
more fully emphasize two phases of sponsorship we will differentiate between "Carrying
the Message" and "Working with Others."

"Working with Others," commonly referred
to as "Sponsorship," is the art of helping an
alcoholic to arrest his illness.

Sponsorship amounts to a pact between two
alcoholics in which one, admitting he is powerless over alcohol, requests help and supervision from the other, an A.A. member, who
in turn agrees that he will devote his best effort to help the other make the A.A. philosophy his *"Way of Life."**

Sponsorship has to do with human life and
* Read paragraph 3, page 108, in the book, "ALCOHOL-
ICS ANONYMOUS."

happiness. It is a serious endeavor best accomplished by experienced members with
good examples of contented sobriety. We
work with alcoholics to immunize ourselves
against drinking and to help them recover
from alcoholism. Newcomers will do well to
team up with older members in carrying on
this work.

The member who sponsors carries the message, but the member who carries the message
does not necessarily sponsor.

By this we wish to imply that a member who
has been in Alcoholics Anonymous thirty days
can carry the message to other alcoholics, but
he surely would not attempt to help straighten
out another man's thinking, or sponsor him
when he does not yet understand his own
problem.

The question naturally arises, "What con-
stitutes carrying the message to alcoholics, how
far do we go in this respect?"

The list of suggested methods is not complete but will provide examples and at the
same time serve as a basis of comparison for
other ways that you may have in mind:

    1. The most convincing message you can pre-
       sent to intimate associates with alcoholic

problems is your own normal contented sobriety.

This statement rules out the theory that the exhibitionist who seeks out his old drinking cronies to show them he can indulge in soft drinks all night, is an approved method of carrying the message.

We hold with the advice given by our founders in this respect. They say, "Assuming that we are spiritually fit, we can do all sorts of things alcoholics are not supposed to do." You will note that we have made an important qualification, therefore, ask yourself on each occasion, "Have I any good social, business, or personal reason for going to this place, or am I stealing a little vicarious pleasure from the atmosphere of such places? . . . But be sure that you are on solid spiritual ground before you start and that your motive in going is thoroughly good."*

2. Admitting to someone that you are an alcoholic.

3. The story of your A.A. experience to professional men whom you know intimately, such as doctors, lawyers, judges, also men of the clergy.

* Read pages 113 and 114 in the book, "ALCOHOLICS ANONYMOUS."

4. Calls with older members who are sponsoring.
5. The example of regular attendance at A.A. meetings. This includes out-of-town meetings when traveling.
6. By becoming part of the group and assuming responsibility.
7. By assuming the responsibility of talking before A.A. groups if asked to help out with a program.
8. By your obvious belief that you have received help from a *Power Greater than Yourself*.
9. Hospital calls.
10. Telephone calls to new members.
11. Personal talks with members after meetings, particularly new members.
12. Talks with wives or relatives who are interested and ask for an understanding of how some member of their family might be benefited.
13. By the practice of tolerance and understanding of weaker members' problems which you attempt to help them overcome by constructive word or action.
14. By close observance and study of our Twelve-step Program as a means of qualifying for sponsorship.

15. By making a reasonable pledge of your time, money and energy.
16. By owning one or more books that you read yourself and lend to new members.
17. Distribution of our literature to interested people.
18. By advising all new members to own the big A.A. Book.

THIRD DIVISION

*"And to practice these principles in all our affairs."**

The principles of the Twelve Steps sum up to a logical practical philosophy that, when willingly and honestly lived, guarantees any alcoholic recovery from his illness.

Recovery is all that we can expect or ask for as we know that an alcoholic can never practice controlled drinking because his nervous system is not constituted to permit it.

The quest of the human race is sane behavior, useful endeavor, security, peace of mind, and happiness. This is our rightful inheritance, but one which is denied the alcoholic so long as he fails to recognize in alcoholism a three-fold illness.

* Read pages 165 to 179 inclusive in the book, "ALCOHOLICS ANONYMOUS."

His heritage is restored to him:

1. When he acknowledges his illness.
2. When he seeks help from a *Power Greater than Himself* to arrest it.
3. When he studies and isolates his moral defects of character.
4. When he admits these defects to himself, God, and another human being.
5. When he realizes the physical, mental, and spiritual injury these defects have caused.
6. When he concedes the injury his self-centered drinking addiction has inflicted upon others.
7. When he asks God to forgive him for these injuries and is willing to make amends to those harmed.
8. When, having achieved happiness, sane behavior, and useful living through sobriety, he maintains it by a daily checkup on his progress and continues the conscious contact he has established with God.
9. When he shares the knowledge and experience of his recovery from alcoholism with other alcoholics who ask for help.
10. When he continues the practice of these principles in *All His Affairs.*

WORKING WITH OTHERS*

A.A. usage of the word sponsorship has evolved from the rehabilitative work recovered A.A. members have done with other alcoholics.

The following quotation from the book "Alcoholics Anonymous" commends this service by a frank statement from our Founders. "Practical experience shows that nothing will so much insure immunity from drinking as intensive work with other alcoholics. It works when other activities fail."

A.A. groups are in agreement with this advice. They have been quick to realize their need for Twelve Step work. It not only "insures immunity from drinking;" it is the life blood of A.A., the motivating factor of our growth. By zealous, humble effort the members of our fellowship have established strong chapters throughout the world. Favorable publicity has helped new groups in the making and increased the larger ones.

Sponsorship stands out as a most important, integrating function to the welfare and stability of all A.A. members.

* See page 101 in the book, "ALCOHOLICS ANONYMOUS."

Today's sponsorship problems, although easier in many respects, present complexities that did not confront our Founders. We are obligated to thousands of alcoholics who have entrusted their lives in our hands asking for competent supervision of their recovery from alcoholism. Our response, although diversified in procedure, has met this demand with tangible evidence of success which can be measured in terms of reclaimed lives, health, sanity and contented sobriety.

Of necessity there has been variance in group ideology, in success, in approach and indoctrination. However, the record of accomplishment by Alcoholics Anonymous is the only world-wide record of *Mass Recovery from Alcoholism*. To consider our enviable accomplishment is to concede a job well done. To apply A.A. philosophy, however, is to ask God's help for improvement. Where have we been lax in those cases that failed? Have we fallen short of the sponsorship suggestions so providentially placed in our hands by our Founders?

Since the book, "Alcoholics Anonymous," contains a successful, proved method of both approaching and working with other alcohol-

149

ics, we believe it should be adopted for more universal application.

Does it seem unwise to contemplate the benefits A.A. could gain by unified acceptance of an orthodox interpretation of the chapter "Working with Others?" Would it not simplify sponsorship and aid the newcomer if the "Gin Hound" from Manhattan and the "Alky" from California met on the same general grounds of sponsorship procedure? Shouldn't we place more emphasis on our need for such achievement?

Many will honestly answer that they are already doing this. Some see no reason for it. Others are indifferent. Members who visit many A.A. groups in their travels report the need of a standard outline for sponsorship activities. Since we have the outline in the book, "Alcoholics Anonymous," perhaps we should meditate our great need for its general acceptance.

It is easy to sit back and believe that there is nothing we can do about this, or to arrive at the conclusion that each group is too well entrenched in its own ideologies to make changes. Is this rationalization or is it the truth? Do we wish to improve our A.A. service to the prospective member or will we settle for the job we are doing? Are we right or are we wrong? No one is to judge but ourselves.

Step Ten suggests that if we are wrong we admit it, and promptly. This brings up other questions pertaining to organized groups sponsoring younger groups. Are we obligated to pass on the "Know-How" of sponsorship to them or should we let them learn the "Hard Way?" Should we offset "Frothy Emotional Appeal" with example and sound A.A. instruction and advise them to surrender self-centeredness and start practicing Step Twelve as our Founders recommended it? Many of us work with other groups. Have we questioned our motives? Do we seek personal recognition or are we humbly trying to bring understanding and help to them? These and other questions form the basis upon which we judge our own A.A. progress. Again we alone are the judges.

Sponsorship stripped of all controversial issues has two purposes. *One*. It helps us to keep sober. *Two*. It helps other alcoholics arrest their alcoholism. Our examples of contented sobriety give them strong recovery incentive. How we sponsor is a personal matter. A.A. does not dictate; we alone decide. The fact we make a call merely to keep ourselves sober has its rewards. Our chances for sobriety might be greater, however, if we followed through with complete sponsorship.

Those of us who engage in sponsorship change our pattern of procedure with experience which we enlarge upon from day to day. The sage wisdom that was ours at three months is hardly adequate a few months or years later. Many of us are soon willing to agree that sponsorship under terms other than those described in the chapters, "Working with Others," "The Doctor's Opinion," "There Is a Solution," "We Agnostics" and "More About Alcoholism," falls far short of success. When we follow these chapters we have success with our prospects; when we deviate we invite A.A. headaches. If this is true, we find a simple answer in the study of these chapters.

Failure to help those to whom we "Carry the Message" makes us two time losers. We lessen the prospect's immediate chance for recovery and lose the benefits of working with them. Checking ourselves we often wonder why we failed. Did our emotions over the family plight obscure our knowledge of the fatal, incurable malady of our alcoholic prospect? Did we try to rush him in for the family's sake? Did we fail through lack of information about our prospect? Were we trying to administer A.A. therapy to a person whose basic illness was other than alcoholism? Do we believe that all alcoholics can recover? Our answers to these and other questions are to be found in the Big Book, "Alcoholics Anonymous."

For members who are interested in further consideration of the matter, the following list of thought-provoking questions may prove helpful. No attempt to answer them has been made except by reference to pages, paragraphs and lines in the book, "Alcoholics Anonymous." We realize the list does not comprise complete sponsorship data, but believe that it touches on many fundamentals. We hope it may prompt you to enlarge upon your fund of A.A. knowledge by reviewing the advice our founders have given us for "Working with Others."

"Carrying the Message to Alcoholics" has general acceptance as good A.A. procedure. Prior to the founding of A.A. what was its influence? (Answers) Page 19, pars. 1-2-3-

4-5; Page 20, par. 5; Page 26, par. 2; Pages 21-22-23-24; Pages 168-169; Page 191, pars. 1-2.

What is the importance of sponsorship to our recovery from alcoholism? Can it be considered a "Must" in A.A.? (Answers) Page 101, pars. 2-3; Page 24, par. 4; Page 24, par. 5; Page 106, par. 1; Page 109, par. 2; Page 114, par. 2, lines 11-12-13.

Our fellowship has earned a splendid record of reclaiming the lives of alcoholics. Does this imply that all alcoholics who ask for help can recover? (Answers) Page 178, par. 1; Page 70, par. 1.

What of our future membership; from what source will they come; how are we to contact them? (Answers) Page 101, par. 3, lines 1-2-3; Page 169, pars. 1-2; Page 170, pars. 4-5; Page 176, par. 2; Page 177, pars. 1-2-3-4; Page 252, par. 4; Page 262, par. 1, lines 8-9-10-11-12-13; Page 270, pars. 1-2; Page 279, par. 2; Page 293, par. 1; Page 312, pars. 1-2-3-4; Page 392, par. 1.

How essential are our examples of contented sobriety to the alcoholic seeking help from A.A.? (Answers) Page 28, pars. 3-4-5;

Page 101, par. 1, lines 5-6; Page 101, par. 3, lines 8-9; Page 192, par. 2, lines 13-14-15-16-17-18; Page 248, par. 5; Page 249, pars. 1-2.

Some prospective members toy with the idea of controlled drinking or are undecided if they are alcoholic. Does the "Big Book" recommend a procedure or offer a test by which they may determine their condition? (Answers) Page 43, par. 1; Page 42, par. 2.

When, if ever, do we drop a prospective member? (Answers) Page 102, par. 1; Page 108, par. 2; Page 273, par. 1; Page 106, par. 1.

What is the requirement for membership in A.A.? (Answers) Page 7, par. 5, lines 3-4; in the chapter "Foreword."

Is our program for those other than alcoholics? (Answers) Under chapter "Foreword"; Page 7, par. 1; Page 36, par. 1; Page 40, par. 1; Page 41; Page 42, par. 1; Page 72, No. 12; Page 104, par. 2; Page 108, par. 2, lines 2-3.

What is the value of our stories to newcomers? (Answers) Page 249, pars. 1-2-3-4-5; Page 253, pars. 1-2; Page 53, par. 2; Page 104, par. 1.

What is the first step of an alcoholic's recovery? (Answer) Page 41, par. 2.

How important is hospitalization to an alcoholic's recovery? (Answers) Page 2, last par.; Page 252-253; Page 4, par. 1; Page 103, par. 1, lines 4-5; Page 389, last par.; Page 390, pars. 1-2-3.

When we find a prospect for Alcoholics Anonymous what is the exact procedure for handling him? What steps do we take? (Answers) Pages 102, 103, 104, 105, 106, 107, 108, 109, 110, 111, 112, 113.

What about the physical condition of our prospect; does it have much to do with his recovery? (Answers) Page 2, pars. 1-2; Page 101, par. 1, line 7; Page 102, par. 1, lines 5-6; Page 104, par. 3; Page 146, last par.; Page 147, pars. 1-2-3.

Do we need information relative to our prospect's background, religion, drinking pattern and the seriousness of his condition? If we do where should we get it? (Answer) Page 102, par. 1-2.

Do we always try to stop our man from a binge or is it sometimes best that he goes on another one? (Answer) Page 102, par. 3.

Do we deal with alcoholics when they are very drunk or ugly? (Answer) Page 102, par. 3, lines 3-4-5-6-7-8.

Do we ever force ourselves upon an alcoholic and insist he stop drinking? (Answers) Page 102, par. 4; Page 42, Par. 2.

Do we call upon a man when he is jittery and depressed? (Answer) Page 103, par. 2.

What is the best policy relative to seeing our man. Do we talk to him in the presence of his family? (Answer) Page 103, par. 2-3.

When do we refer to alcoholism as a sickness? A fatal malady? (Answer) Page 104, pars. 2-3.

What about mention of spiritual matters? Should we make free mention of A.A.'s spiritual features? (Answers) Page 105, lines 10-11; Page 57, pars. 3-4.

Regarding religion. Do we discuss it with our prospect? (Answers) Page 105, pars. 1-2; Page 106, 1st 9 lines.

Supposing our prospect is a real alcoholic who shows interest in joining A.A. Do we lend him our book? (Answer) Page 107, line 6.

Assume that he seems too anxious to get into our membership at once. What action do we take? (Answer) Page 107, par. 1.

Some newcomers expect us to act as their wet nurses and bankers; is this recommended A.A. practice? (Answer) Page 107, par. 2.

What suggestions are given by our Founders for reading the book, "Alcoholics Anonymous?" Is the newcomer advised to read it before he comes into our fellowship? (Answer) Page 107, last par.

It is easy to become discouraged with alcoholics who do not respond. How do we meet this condition? (Answer) Page 108, par. 2.

What discretion should we observe when helping a person who is homeless and broke? (Answer) Page 109, par. 1.

When, if ever, do we let alcoholics live in our homes? (Answers) Page 109, last par.; Page 110, lines 1-2.

Divorce and separation are often encountered. What if our man believes he cannot recover until his family is united? (Answer) Page 112, first 18 lines.

What example besides contented sobriety do we owe those we work with? (Answer) Page 112, par. 2.

Is it wise for a sponsor to participate in the new members' family quarrels? (Answers) Page 112, last par.; Page 113, par. 2.

How does the new member meet circumstances that require his presence at bars, night clubs or homes where liquor is served? (Answers) Page 113, pars. 2-3-4; Pages 114, 115.

WE DON'T HAVE TO—BUT . . .

The obligation recovery from alcoholism imposes is paid to God, our families and society by our willing practice of daily A.A. living. This practice, though restrictive, rewards us in hourly dividends of sobriety, service to others, security and happiness for our families. As we have grown in understanding we have come to realize that voluntarily we have placed a number of "Musts" in our everyday living. They have become a part of our new A.A. personalities which we have willingly embraced. We are surprised to find ourselves so unopposed to conditions which formerly we regarded as impossible.

You may be interested in checking some of these voluntary "Musts" which are to be found in the book, "Alcoholics Anonymous." Many of them relate to sponsorship, others to our emotional conduct and spiritual phases of our program. Direct quotations have been supplanted by reference to pages, paragraphs and lines. We offer them as noteworthy milestones to achievement in A.A. living.

1. It relates to physical illness. Page 2, par. 1, line 5.

WE DON'T HAVE TO—BUT . . .

2. Self-centeredness. Page 74, par. 2, line 5.
3. Self-destruction. Page 74, par. 2, line 5.
4. Resentments. Page 79, par. 2, line 7.
5. Sex. Page 82, par. 2, line 1.
6. Amends. Page 82, par. 2, line 2.
7. Honesty. Page 86, par. 1, line 1.
8. Step Five. Page 86, par. 1, line 1.
9. Excusing ourselves. Page 86, par. 2, line 9.
10. Procrastination. Page 87, line 5.
11. Creditors—Fear. Page 90, last par., last line.
12. Courage. Page 91, par. 2, line 8.
13. Duty. Page 92, par. 2, line 4.
14. Keep sober. Page 94, last par., line 4.
15. Reconstruction. Page 95, par. 2, line 2.
16. Behavior—Memory. Page 95, par. 3, line 6.
17. "Vision of God's Will." Page 98, lines 1-2-3.
18. "Proper use of the will." Page 98, lines 4-5-6.
19. Spiritual improvement. Page 98, par. 1, line 7.
20. Avoiding worry. Page 98, last par., line 9.
21. Sponsorship. Page 101, par. 2, line 4.
22. Family help. Page 103, top, line 4.
23. Vital faith. Page 105, last par.
24. Decision. Page 107, last par.
25. Finding God. Page 108, line 2.
26. Harm or argument. Page 111, par. 1, line 12.
27. Repair damage. Page 111, par. 2, line 7.

28. Divorce. Page 112, line 3.
29. Sponsor's duty. Page 112, par. 2, line 1.
30. Wives—Dissension. Page 131, par. 1, line 7.
31. Demanding wives. Page 131, par. 3, line 2.
32. Family criticism. Page 140, par. 1, line 4.
33. Facing responsibility. Page 140, par. 2, line 3.
34. Assuming blame. Page 141, line 1.
35. Keep spiritually active. Page 170, par. 4, line 3.
36. Self-preservation. Page 173, par. 2, line 6.
37. Starting a Group. Page 178, par. 2, line 3.

Recovery from alcoholism is possible to alcoholics providing they want to get well and free themselves from reservations. "Willingness, honesty and open-mindedness are the essentials of recovery. But these are indispensable." Such are the closing words of the book, "Alcoholics Anonymous." We believe that close study of this book and adherence to its principles are the greatest assets to our success in the A.A. fellowship.

Twice Born Books

For twice born Men and Women

WHEN MAN LISTENS: Everyone can listen to God by
Cecil Rose and Carl Tuchy Palmieri
"When Man Listens" was written in 1938 by Cecil Rose,
an Oxford Group member. Many of the concepts
described in this book found their way into the Big
Book. "When Man Listens", also found its way into both
Dr Bob and Bill W's Libraries. It was required reading
for the early Akron A.A. groups. It is considered by
many to be the mini A.A. book, as it reads like the Big
Book. A must read for anyone who wants to deepen
his/her connection with God.

The Conversion of the Church by Samuel M. Shoemaker
and Carl Tuchy Palmieri
"The Genius of Fellowship" was written in 1932 By Sam
Shoemaker. Bill W. the cofounder of A.A stated that
Sam was the third cofounder of A.A. that "He was one
of the few without whose ministration A.A. could never
have been born in the first place nor prospered since"
"From his teachings, Dr Bob and I absorbed most of the
principles of A.A. Our ideas of self-examination,
acknowledgement of character defects, restitution for
harms done, and working with others came straight from
Sam" "He passed to us the spiritual keys by which so
many of us have since been liberated". The book has an
entire section on the Genius of Fellowship, He Begins
the chapter with a definition of Fellowship. "Fellowship
In the spiritual sense means the intimacy which springs

up between human beings who are agreed as touching a spiritual ideal which they are working out together". "Second only after the hunger for God, comes the hunger for comradeship with others who are hungry for God." The Fellowship of Alcoholics Anonymous carries on this spiritual meaning.

In his concluding remarks, Sam states" We have taken what is meant to be a spiritual family fellowship and turned it into a business organization. If we are to turn it back again, it can be done in no wholesale way. No reorganization will do it, no campaign of mass-evangelism, no quick and easy remedies. The cure lies in the rediscovery of fellowship under the guidance of God's Holy Spirit. Again we see that the fellowship of Alcoholics Anonymous   is based on this premise and principle. Tradition # 2 states "For our group purpose there is but one ultimate authority - a loving God as he may express himself in our group conscience" tradition # 8 states "Alcoholics Anonymous should remain forever nonprofessional"   The first century Christian church was called the fellowship. The Oxford Group, In the United States was also called the fellowship. Today Alcoholics Anonymous is called the fellowship. It was Sam's fellowship that flourished in the 20's and 30's and was Bill W.'s original fellowship
Sam Shoemaker brought The Oxford Group movement to the United States In 1918 and was the National leader of the movement until 1940. Ebby T., and Bill W., Found their recovery Under Sam's direction in 1934 and 35

To Drink or Not to Drink: The Common Sense of Drinking by Carl Tuchy Palmieri and Richard R. Peabody

The book was written in 1928. And stands today as one of the most important contributions to problem drinkers. The purpose of the book is to define the alcoholic, show how he/she arrived at this condition, and by what method one can rid him/her of his/her habit once and for all. While aimed at the chronic inebriate the book will, be of interest to all who drink, more especially as it may show them where they stand on the line that separates moderation from excess. We find many parallels with and similar thinking to The Book Alcoholics Anonymous.

Both speak of the critical importance of Honesty. In The common sense of Drinking, Richard Peabody states "once the alcoholic takes up treatment, he must be absolutely honest in giving account of his thoughts and actions, and he must take great precautions against lying ingeniously (rationalizing) to himself. To Be Frank and honest in all relations especially in all relations with oneself, is the first principle of mental hygiene. In the Chapter How it works we find the following petition. "those who do not recover are people who cannot or will not give themselves to this simple program, usually men and women who are constitutionally incapable of being honest with themselves" "They are naturally incapable of grasping and developing a manner of living that demands vigorously honesty" "There are those, too who suffer from grave emotional and mental disorders, but many of them do recover if they have the capacity to be honest"

Both books speak of the importance of literature Peabody writes It is often helpful in influencing the trend of thinking to read books of a constructive nature whether they bear directly on the problem or whether they the appeal is through inference." "Books which influence this manner are biographies and autobiographies of men who have become successful" The big book speaks of literature in the Chapter into action "we sometimes select and memorize a few select prayers which emphasize the principles we have been discussing. There are many helpful books also. Suggestions about these may be obtained from one's priest, minister, or Rabbi"

Writing is recommended in both the big book and "To Drink or Not to Drink".

The big book references writing in the 12 steps. "In dealing with resentments we set them on paper" "made a list of all the people we had harmed" In Bill's story we have bills stating "We, made a list of people I had hurt or toward whom I felt resentment" step # 8 made a list of all the people we had harmed, and became willing to make amends to them all etc.

Reading and writing is outlined in the common sense of drinking as a necessary step to cure alcoholism. "Writing as well as reading is of benefit to the patient. It helps crystallize in his mind the idea he has received"
"One of the tasks I set is the making of a daily schedule, which once made out had to be lived up to."

<u>Inspired Children</u> by Tuchy Palmieri and Olive M. Jones This book presents the first detailed description of the influence of the Oxford Group movement (In America called A First Century Christian Fellowship) upon the lives of children. One of the extraordinary things that the movement does is to deal with all people upon the basis of their own personal need. Part one is filled with true stories of children's spiritual experience, and how using the principles of the program gave them a personal and loving God. Part two titled "the way, how children learn to know God." tell us how prayer, quiet time with subsequent sharing, stories, and literature are the tools used as the pathway to finding their personal God. This book proves that what worked with adults in the Oxford Group was just as effective with children. That leads to the conclusion that what works for Adults in A.A. will also work for children. It is Heartwarming, uplifting and badly needed.

<u>Life Changers: 13th Edition</u> by Harold Begbie and <u>Carl Tuchy Palmieri</u>

Life Changers is first and foremost about how one man, Frank Buchman changed the lives of millions of people throughout the world. The Oxford Group as his work had come to be known was the most successful worldwide Christian movement of the 20th Century the power of his work is highlighted by heartwarming stories of rebirth and recovery of the young men of the Oxford Group in England... Many of the Oxford Groups, founding principles, (confidence, confession, conviction, conversion and continuance)   live on today within the fellowship of Alcoholics Anonymous. The stories told in life changers are as powerful as those told in the A.A. big book, with the notable exception that they cover the full gambit of maladies. It also validates the second half of the 12th step. That bringing the principles of the program to all your affairs works as well as is does for the malady of Alcoholism

Twice Born Men: A Clinic of Regeneration by Harold Begbie and Carl Tuchy Palmieri
The purpose of this book is to bring home the fact that "conversion is the only means by which a radically bad person can be changed into a radically good person. The fact stands clear and unassailable that with conversion, a person consciously wrong, inferior, and unhappy, becomes consciously right, superior, and happy. It produces not a change, but a revolution in character .It does not alter, it creates a new personality. Men who have been irretrievably bad, under conversion have become ardent savers of the lost. Written in 1909, it contains heartwarming stories of rebirth and recovery during the later part of the 19th Century. The principles that guide the Salvation Army of today were put down during late 1800's. Many of the same principles are guiding the members of Alcoholics Anonymous today. A number of Recovering alcoholics from the A.A, fellowship have turned to The Salvation Army for More spiritual support and for additional service work. The concept of helping others with the same or similar

problem, had it birthplace with the Salvationists taking a man off the streets, changing his life, and having him serve to change the lives of others lives on today in the Salvation Army. It has gotten stronger and farther reaching since its inception in the mid 1800's

Twice Born Ministers: We Are All Ministers by Samuel M. Shoemaker and Carl "Tuchy" Palmieri

Twice Born Ministers was written in 1929 by Sam Shoemaker. He dedicated the book Twice Born Ministers, to Frank Buchman who he considered a Minister of Jesus Christ and leader of his fellowship. Through this little book a dozen men in ministry are saying to us, whether   we are ministers or laypeople, that a great thing happened to them which can also happen to us—something which did not destroy but fulfilled and enriched their former religious convictions and experiences, which helped them in knowing how to meet peoples deepest needs, and freed them from innumerable burdens which they used to carry. The deepest mark of reality upon these stories is the radiant spiritual joy which shines through them. It is only the truth that makes men free. Sam was committed to The Oxford Group Fellowship, To the Fellowship of Alcoholics anonymous, and to the Church as a vehicle to support men and women in their pursuit of a personal God through being reborn. Sam has been acknowledged by Bill Wilson as the 3rd co-founder of A.A.

The Foundations of A.A. by Carl Tuchy Palmieri
A compilation of three books Written at different times
yet when read together they present the most complete
picture of the foundational elements of the Alcoholics
Anonymous movement. Twice born Men (1909),
Life Changers written in 1923 both written by Harold
Begbie and Children of the second birth written in 1927
by Sam Shoemaker must read for people wanting to
know the essence of the miracle of the program, and how
A.A. stands on the foundations of two modern day
movements - The Salvationists and The Oxford Group
One will also get a clear picture of The work that Sam in
his ministry did to clarify the process of recovery and
rebirth for later use in Alcoholics Anonymous.

Children of the Second Birth: What We Used to Be Like,
What Happened, and What We Are Like Now by
Samuel M. Shoemaker and Carl Palmieri

'Children of the second birth were written in 1927 and
are filled with stories of men and women who found God
and recovered from various maladies.
The primary focus was on quiet time—finding God's
will and helping others to do the same. The daily focus
was what the Oxford Group called "Quiet Time. The
distinguishing element of Quiet Time is listening for the
guidance of God. The validity of God's guidance shows
itself by more acute moral perception, more genuine
human relationships, and increasing assurance of what
one ought to do with every hour of the day. This is an
excellent modern day example of the effectiveness of the

Oxford Group principles on the lives of ordinary people in all walks of life.

The Original 12 Step Book
Written In 1946, By Ed Webster (The little red Book) was the first guide used to help people do the twelve steps. It was approved by AA, promoted, by Dr Bob; Dr. Bob thought it was the best description of how to work the steps that had ever been written. He sent copies of it all over the U.S. and Canada with his recommendation. Until Dr. Bob's death in 1950, he insisted that the New York A.A. office make copies of this book available for sale through their office. And it was offered for sale by AA prior to AA 12 & 12. It remains as the clearest and easiest to understand guide.

The Game of Life

This prosperity classic was written in 1925 by Florence Scovil Shinn. It stands today as one of the all time great classics that has helped people through the generations to find prosperity. Our golden classic (50th Reprint) contains original material not found in other reprints. This edition uses bold print all throughout the book to emphasize the Authors point.

Turning Fear into Power

""Turning Fear into power", was written by Richard lynch in 1932

It provides straight forward strategies to overcome fear in all facets of life. This is a one of a kind edition. It has been enhanced by writings added along the margins to strengthen the relevant points made by Lynch. Grace M. Bosworth would strengthen each important point made by Lynch, sometimes just quoted words of wisdom, passages from the bible, or excerpts from other well known works. She was indeed a learned person and she knew what and where to insert her words to bring home the point being made in the book. This never before seen edition is now available for today's generation who are seeking freedom from fear.

Recovery Books

Off The Wall Contrarian quotes for people in Recovery

The goal of this book is to provide the person working with an Alcohol Problem, more Tips, tactics and tools to strengthen recovery (I am a recovering Alcoholic Sobriety date April 14th 1986)

This book is a collection of poignant, touching, and truthful thoughts and phrases related to the recovery process. Inspired by AA's 12-step program, this book provides hope and inspiration for anyone dealing with addiction and substance abuse issues. As with material presented in and around the rooms, it is suggested that you take what works and leave the rest. What does not work today may work for you tomorrow, which is why it is a good idea to pick up the book as often as you can. Program tools are a key to many people's recovery and this book gives you an opportunity to use several tools. 1) Reading recovery literature. 2) Writing- takes a quote each day, write it down and carry it with you. 3) Meditation- by pondering or meditating on a quote you can improve your conscious contact with God. 4) Telephone- sharing a quote with a friend helps both. 5) Anonymity- many of the quotes and healing writings are from unknown authors. May their anonymity help you in your time of need?

The Food Contrarian

A book filled with tips, tactics and tools to help people with eating issues. It utilizes the 12 steps as a foundation and brings fresh ideas and strategies to assist the compulsive eater or non eater- (I lost two brothers form food related illnesses. I am also a grateful recovering compulsive overeater. In The program since March of 1991)

This book is a collection of poignant, touching, and truthful thoughts and phrases related to recovery from eating disorders or other food addictions. Inspired by AA's 12-step program, this book provides hope and inspiration for anyone dealing with food-related issues. 1) A dishonest mistake-- a lie. 2) Some people do the steps by sidestepping. 3) Count your blessings instead of counting your calories. 4) DIET: Doing Insane Eating Temporarily. 5) For the anorexic too little is too much. NOT FOR STUDY PURPOSES LIGHT READING WITH SERIOUS PONDERING Suggestion: Read one or two per day, write them down on a piece of paper and post or carry with you. 1) Relapse: When your disease is in recovery. 2) Binge: When enough is not enough. 3) Purge: An attempt to correct a mistake with another mistake. 4) Bulimia: Two wrongs to make right.

Relationship Recovery

This book is all encompassing and is suggested for anyone working a 12 step program of any kind as it is most likely that the problem has its roots in relationship to a greater or lesser degree.

RELATIONSHIP RECOVERY is about using the 12-step program principles to help anyone suffering from relationship ills. While not approved by any 12-step program, it is a great addition to the literature offered to help in doing the steps, especially steps 3 through 12.

Resolving relationship issues is the foundational key to any 12-step program, and recovery cannot occur without addressing it. This workbook is intended to help people in that endeavor.

Why Not Try God

The story of a man who found himself addicted to drug and alcohol and how he found recovery in the 12 step program. How he used program principles in all his affairs. Kreige suffered from mental disorders and used the principle of vigorous honesty that enabled him to lead a normal life. In addition the book has articles from Sam shoemaker, Emmet Fox, Sybil   Partridge and James Allen

Inspirational/Motivational books

Tuchy's Law

 Tuchy's Law is a collection of quotes that spoke to me over a 40 year period from 1960 to 2000. The quotes covered all aspects of life and were from my point of view wise words. A few famous people, but mostly the people in my life that crossed my path

TUCHY'S LAW AND OTHER CONTRARIAN QUOTES TO HELP YOU IN LIFE'S JOURNEY is a life-affirming and thought-provoking collection of quips, quotes, and proverbs that were gathered and honed by the author and his family, friends, and colleagues over a 25-year period. Covering topics as diverse as ambition, success, initiative, and handling setbacks, the more than one thousand warm and witty sayings in this book will bring a smile to your face and leave you nodding in recognition.

The platinum Rule and other Contrarian Quotes

This is a collection of contrarian quotes many Fields contrarian quote was "If at first you do not succeed, try again, then give up and don't make a fool of yourself.

Another is The Platinum rule "do unto others as they would have you do unto them" these were gathered over the same 40 year period

THE PLATINUM RULE AND OTHER CONTRARIAN SAYINGS is a warm, witty, and life-affirming collection of quips, quotes, and aphorisms that will touch your heart and bring a smile to your face. Gathered and honed by the author over a 40-year period, the 522 sayings in this book will bring back fond memories on the topics of family, work, self-worth, dealing with adversity, aging gracefully, and many, many more.

Josephine in Her Words.

Josephine in Her words is a collection of words of Wisdom and related comments that Mom had given us over the last 60 years. It was a 90th birthday gift to Mom. The reviews on mom's book started what I refer to as interactive books/workbook

I essence it was a method of enabling the reader record any thoughts desires and memories that came about while reading the quotes and words of wisdom.

Phil in His Words Our Dad

An interactive book that enables the reader to write down words of wisdom from his /her dads that were triggered as the wisdom words of my Dad was read. Writing is an excellent way to bring back a deceased parent. Dad had been gone 15 years when this book was created. The source of the book was from several people who knew dad. As an experiment we took The Grandchildren and the Great Grandchildren that were too young to remember dad, and read highlights of the book to them. The result was phenomenal. Dad was transformed from being just a picture on the wall to a real person who had passed down ways of being to there Moms/Dads and grandparents

The words and wisdom of a devoted father collected and recorded by a loving son, PHIL, IN HIS WORDS: OUR DAD will resonate with adult children of all ages and backgrounds who remember and appreciate the gifts given to them by their parents. So often it is the wisdom of our fathers, grandfathers, mothers, and grandmothers that encouraged us to take the right path in life. The reading of Phil's words may trigger the words that were given to you, the reader. You are encouraged to write them down to reflect on, to pass on to your children, and to share with friends. You are encouraged to write down your favorite words to pass on to future generations. Enjoy Phil's words and may they help you in some way.

Sex and Intimacy

A serious and yet light hearted book of tactics, techniques and tools to make relationships work better. It approaches sex and Intimacy with great words of wisdom from people in all walks of life. Many words brought humor and lightness to this hard and hot topic

The words in Sex and Intimacy: The Gifts of Life are given by wise men, famous people, and common folks and are intended to give the reader truisms, advice, and comfort in the areas of sex and intimacy. It is our belief that sex and intimacy are God-given gifts to be enjoyed as any other gift. We also believe that the healthier people's sex lives are, the happier and healthier people are in all aspects of life. Recent research verifies the benefits of having sex on a regular basis. Sex can be fun, exciting, and a great way to become closer with your partner. Sex can also be great for your health, since your sexual health and mental well-being are closely linked. You are encouraged to use this interactive book to jot down and record ideas which, when implemented, would make your sex life healthier and happier.

Money and So much more- The real meaning of wealth

A book filled with wisdom from the famous and not so famous from ancient times and from current times. Again the goal of the book is to inspire people to put money in its right place, not have it rule them and how to be wise with money

MONEY AND SO MUCH MORE: THE TRUE MEANING OF WEALTH is designed to shift a person's relationship to money so that it no longer brings upset and worry. This is achieved by using quotes, proverbs, famous sayings, anonymous words, and humor. In addition, the book is interactive, and the reader is encouraged to put into writing his or her thoughts and actions as they relate to money. Through these words the reader is moved to be different in the world and that money will take its appropriate place in life, thus allowing one to be free of money's grip.

Oprah in Her Words- our American Princess

Many of Oprah's wise words are enhanced by the Addition of Suggested affirmations, inquiries, and suggested action. The Goal of the book is to Make Oprah's words personal to the reader by giving suggestions and allowing interactivity through writing in the book in the appropriate space.

Tuchy Palmieri's interactive and inspiring book Oprah, In Her Words: Our American Princess is filled with quotes from Oprah Winfrey expanded to include suggested affirmations, inquiries, and actions. Readers are given space in which to create or to take on their own affirmations, inquiries, and actions. The book is divided into challenging topics with words designed to inspire, encourage, and assist.

Obama in His Words- pre -Election

Filled with the quotes, speeches and words that he used that helped him win the election. The Goal of the book was to go beyond the pictures and create a historical keepsake of his words

This dynamic, interactive workbook shares with the reader the words Barack Obama gave us before and during his campaign; words that moved, inspired, and touched many of us. They collectively propelled him into the White House as the 44th President of the United States. May this collection of words serve as the beginning of the Obama legacy. He comes to the presidency with one of the highest approval ratings of our modern presidents. May he serve us well. God bless America, and God bless you.

Satisfying Success

This book helps the reader to find the rare space of creating success that satisfies rather than success that is empty

Success is one of the strangest phenomenons in life. First, it is often subjective, and it has been elusive for many as it is often not well defined. Many who work their whole lives finally achieve it, only to find that it is a hollow victory, void of any satisfaction. In this inspiring and thought-provoking book one can discover the paths to satisfying success. You are encouraged to take from the words of others those that resonate for you and leave the ones that do not. You can indeed have both success and satisfaction at the same time. This book proves that it can be done and has been done for others.

To order twice born books

Go to Amazon books, Barnes & Noble or one of many internet book stores for single book orders. For group and multiple book orders go to www.healing-habits.com or Call 203-683-4863 land-line 203-383-0445 CELL

Made in the USA
Middletown, DE
09 March 2021

35092600R00104